8 HABITS *of* LOVE

8 HABITS *of* LOVE

Open Your Heart, Open Your Mind

ED BACON

GRAND CENTRAL
Life & Style
BOSTON • NEW YORK

Copyright © 2012 by J. Edwin Bacon, Jr.
All rights reserved. In accordance with the U.S. Copyright Act of 1976, the scanning, uploading, and electronic sharing of any part of this book without the permission of the publisher is unlawful piracy and theft of the author's intellectual property. If you would like to use material from the book (other than for review purposes), prior written permission must be obtained by contacting the publisher at permissions@hbgusa.com. Thank you for your support of the author's rights.

Grand Central Life & Style
Hachette Book Group
237 Park Avenue
New York, NY 10017

www.HachetteBookGroup.com

Printed in the United States of America

RRD-C

First Edition: September 2012
10 9 8 7 6 5 4 3 2 1

Grand Central Life & Style is an imprint of Grand Central Publishing.
The Grand Central Life & Style name and logo are trademarks of Hachette Book Group, Inc.

The Hachette Speakers Bureau provides a wide range of authors for speaking events. To find out more, go to www.hachettespeakersbureau.com or call (866) 376-6591.

The publisher is not responsible for websites (or their content) that are not owned by the publisher.

Library of Congress Cataloging-in-Publication Data
Bacon, Ed.
8 habits of love : open your heart, open your mind / Ed Bacon. — 1st ed.
p. cm.
Summary: "A spiritual guidebook for living life through love, not fear" — Provided by the publisher.
Includes bibliographical references and index.
ISBN 978-1-4555-0003-1 (regular : alk. paper) 1. Conduct of life. 2. Love — Religious aspects. I. Title. II. Title: Eight habits of love.
BJ1595.B23 2012
241'.4—dc23
2012005516

To Hope
the coeur in my courage

Contents

Introduction

The day Love was illumined,
Lovers learned from You how to burn, Beloved.
The flame was set by the Friend
to give the moth a gate to enter.
Love is a gift from the Beloved to the Lover—

—Abu-Said Abil-Kheir

I invite you on an adventure. It is a lifelong journey that will take you to the deepest, most sacred place within yourself. That powerful inner sanctuary resides in each of us—every human being on earth—and when we access this sanctuary, it grounds us in love, giving us the courage and resilience to stand up to fear. When we open our hearts and minds to love's abundance, we can transform not only our own lives, but also the lives of those around us, making the world a more just, peaceful, and caring place.

It has taken me a lifetime to understand that learning to embrace love and practice its habits at every turn are the deepest responsibilities we have as humans. I invite you to take a place by my side on this long and eventful journey, so that we may travel together, along with many others, toward a better life and a better world.

Those who fly through the sound barrier report that the cockpit shakes the most just before breakthrough. Similarly, the Habits of

Love described in these pages took form for me through some shaky times: deciding to become a minister; leaving the religion of my childhood; working in different parts of the United States with very different congregations; learning to be a father and a grandfather; sharing my life with Hope, my wife. But the first glimpses of what would lead me on this turbulent and wondrous journey came when I was still just a little boy.

We were living in the small town of Jesup, along a historic railway stop in pine-studded, rural Georgia. My father was a Baptist preacher, school principal, and later the county school superintendent, and my mother was a teacher. Our home was a busy and comfortable one, its walls decorated with religious art, its shelves housing countless prized knickknacks. Hanging above the chest of drawers in my childhood bedroom was a simple framed picture of Jesus praying. For 18 years, I laid my head to sleep each night and opened my eyes each morning gazing at this image.

I remember every detail vividly. Jesus, dressed in a humble tunic, kneels in the grass in a lush garden by a rough-hewn boulder, his face open, upturned, and serene. Coming from above is a bright beam of light that bathes his features in warmth. Though he seems to be welcoming that light into himself, his expression suggests that he already knows it exists inside him. He is already home. Infused by the spirit of love, he recognizes the inner sanctuary that allows him to base his life in the force field of love. And so I, too, felt safe and consoled and empowered, night after night, dwelling in the constant light of love and acceptance.

Yet there were other messages I was receiving as a child that contradicted this deep and growing understanding that all humankind is connected by the energy of love. A version of God that I heard preached about from my father's pulpit was one who was wrathful, punitive, and condemning. All around me I saw people who were marginalized and suffering, in particular African Americans, and I often struggled with a sense of inner confusion that left me feeling isolated, unknown and unknowing. There was another image I encountered during those years that only emphasized for me the conflict between these differing experiences of reality.

One summer afternoon, I wandered into my parents' bedroom while they were away. On a table by the window lay the family Bible. The stories inside were illustrated with exquisitely detailed etchings, in all the colors of the rainbow. I loved leafing through the pages and looking at these pictures — except one day when I landed on the pages of the book of Revelation.

There was a glorious green field filled with people. But beneath their feet, the ground was opening up to reveal the orange flames of hell, reaching upward to consume all those who had not been saved. The field was crowded with men, women, and children, some of whom were being lifted up toward light-filled, billowing clouds — these people were supposedly Christ's elect. Others had flames lapping at their ankles and expressions of horror on their faces — these had been denied Christ's love and were destined to burn in hell.

What I remember most clearly was that certain families were torn apart by this division between good and evil, those to be saved and those to be damned. Some children fell to their demise while their happy parents were lifted up. The reverse was also the case. It was traumatizing not only in respect to myself — where would *I* end up? — but also in respect to others I knew and loved. Where would *they* end up? I grasped that even in my small town there were some individuals I knew whom I would never see again, without knowing ahead of time which ones. I felt nauseated, slammed the Bible shut, and ran from the room.

The experience of gazing upon these two imposing, contradictory images of love and fear launched me on my own life-changing journey toward self-discovery, healing, and ministry. It registered in my soul that these two conflicting narratives could not coexist, and that I would have to jettison one in order to fully embrace the other.

After that, in countless seemingly ordinary incidents I began to recognize the critical role of love as a liberating, joy-filled, and guiding force. This growing awareness embedded in me an unshakeable certainty that within each and every human being there lives a core of love and goodness. To be sure, the world and its inhabitants suffer from real evil. Yet at the same time, the world is not divided into persons who are good or evil, blessed or damned. Rather, each of us carries within us a core of sacredness that no evil can damage or distort.

We have the ability to change the course of our lives when we become aware of that core of sacredness—which I call *the Beloved*—and begin to live with it as our guide. Whenever we have a flash of love, innocence, acceptance, inspiration, awe, or wonder, or we're moved to tears or filled with joy, we must remind ourselves: *this is the real me*. We must not let such moments simply pass us by. We must stop and appreciate those moments and act on them—and ask that we receive more of them in the future. This book is my call to you, asking you to embark on this never-ending adventure, as I have done, and take your own steps with this book as your guiding force.

Beneath our wounds and resentments, our fears and insecurities, our neediness and addictions, we are all loved deeply and unconditionally. We therefore each carry within us the capacity to love deeply, unconditionally, and fearlessly. It is through practicing the Habits of Love that we can transform our lives by freeing ourselves from fear. In every concentric circle of human interaction, we can be instruments of bringing people together instead of drawing lines of enmity to separate us.

When we embrace the eight habits I lay out in this book, we recognize that our tired and reflexive responses to our loved ones, and even to strangers, fail to take into consideration their intentions and dreams and our shared goals. We realize that with our children, we can better embrace spontaneity and adventure once we've stepped back from constrictive fears and expectations. In our communities, with our hearts open, we instinctively become less reactive and more responsible. At work, with our minds open, we are less prone to misunderstandings and more likely to feel deeper connections.

Our interactions with others become infused with grace and kindness.

When we employ the energy of love, we are leaving fear behind us and choosing instead to make our way toward a new, inspiring goal: living our lives with open hearts.

The Habits of Love

With this book, I am seeking to meet you exactly where you already are in your life and offer resources so you may find your own answers to the following questions: How do I live the most meaningful life I possibly can? What does that life look like for me? How do I find the voice of courageous creativity within me and trust that voice in the face of harsh realities that swirl around me—and around those I care about? What does this mean for my relationships at home or at work? How do I move forward in my life? How does a family or business or staff or board of directors—or nation, for that matter—leave behind the force field of fear and enter one of love? And what difference does all of this make in the lives of those who are suffering?

This is the tremendous, transformative journey upon which you embark when you embrace these 8 Habits of Love. As immodest as it may sound, it is my earnest hope that over time the Habits of Love will change your life and that of your community in profound and exhilarating ways. I truly believe that by integrating these habits into our daily lives, we make the world a better place. In opening our hearts and our minds, we ultimately change not only ourselves, but also—over time—those around us.

When practiced consistently, these Habits of Love can in fact become habitual and thus change the way we think and behave, fundamentally altering our interactions with those we love most dearly, those we barely know, and with the world at large. They help us see ourselves and those around us with entirely new eyes, as I did when I came to understand that every creature in the world is loved.

In some ways, each Habit of Love is stunningly simple. None requires any deep academic knowledge or religious commitment, but each asks that we look within ourselves so we may open our hearts by identifying and accessing our loved and loving selves. Yet for many, recognizing our inherent goodness—referred to here as the Beloved within or our inner sanctuary—is the most difficult hurdle of all. Each of the eight habits within these pages will offer you the vision, energy, and inspiration to help you make that leap.

The Habit of Generosity is the practice of opening our hearts so we may give and receive. This habit allows every gift that flows into each of us to flow through us to others. In this process we become *affluent* in the real sense of that term. Stillness is the habit in which we experience how richly, completely, and unconditionally each of us is loved and how every other person on the planet is loved in the same way. When we feel lost, frantic, scared, or inadequate, returning to Stillness can restore calm confidence and a vision for the next step. Contrary to what many of us believe, the Habit of Truth is not something we can ever fully possess, but is something that leads us, step by step, during the course of our lifetime. It sheds light on those stories we have inherited from our families, cultures, and religious traditions, and shows us which stories need to be abandoned in order to have an expanded life of freedom.

The Habit of Candor is significant because it is so often misunderstood, yet it is a habit that can be life changing for all the parties involved. It is about having the courage to engage in difficult conversations. In practicing Candor—with those with whom we work and socialize, not only those with whom we are intimate—we deepen our relationships more than we put them at risk. When we are overworked or stressed out, fear breeds like a virus. The joy that comes from allowing the Habit of Play into our lives rescues us from hurting ourselves or others because we were too tense and closed minded.

Forgiveness is something that we do within ourselves as a way of moving forward with our lives. But its benefits are not for us alone. After inviting the Habit of Forgiveness into our lives, our feelings about others and the way we relate to them also change, thereby positively affecting the lives of others within the larger community. Surprisingly to many, the Habit of Forgiveness is, in actuality, about releasing *ourselves*, not others—whereas the Habit of Compassion is about revealing to others the goodness that is inside them. And finally, the Habit of Community teaches us a truth that beats at the very heart of the universe: each of us needs other human beings in order to become fully human. *I am because we are.* We cannot be humane or human alone.

The practice of these eight habits expands the space within us and within our relationships, where love's sacred power can actually be felt overcoming and dispelling fear from inside our being. When love is the summit toward which we are headed, fear is our biggest obstacle. Yet when we open our hearts to love, we are at the same time opening our minds and choosing love over fear as a guiding force. No matter how many inspiring texts, stories, lectures, or sermons we receive, none is as inspiring as discovering the richness of love in our core. I call this love inside all of us *the Beloved*. The 8 Habits of Love outlined in this book help us access that core of love and power within each one of us.

We Are All Beloved

On a Sunday morning some years ago, Ellen introduced herself to me after a worship service. "Good morning. My name is Ellen. I'm Jewish and I thought it important to tell you why I'm here."

As a Christian priest who preaches and celebrates the Eucharist each week at All Saints Episcopal Church, Pasadena, California, I was intrigued. "Please," I said, "go ahead."

"My psychiatrist gave me a prescription to come to church here.

He said that every time you mention 'Jesus,' 'Christ,' or 'Christianity,' I should just bracket those words and focus on what you're saying about *life*."

I was both amazed and delighted. In the same way, rather than write a book on spirituality and religion I have tried to write a book about life. In place of a book about "God," which could be read as some form of theological treatise, I ask you, the reader, to enter into a discussion of a unifying, healing, and encouraging energy that I call the Beloved. Like the word *God*, the Beloved points to something much more profound, mysterious, and life giving than words alone can adequately express.

A wise and dear Muslim friend of mine says, "God does not belong to any religion; every religion belongs to God." The Beloved dwells in every human being and every human being dwells in the Beloved.

Some who hear or read the word *God* are involuntarily flooded with associations—sometimes bad, sometimes good—in their mind, body, and spirit. Too frequently these connotations do not promote either inclusion or reconciliation. Religious history is tragically blemished by practices that hijacked the idea of God for the purpose of creating enemies or infidels, classifying them as evil to justify violence so the group seeking power could be "saved" and ultimately dominate. No wonder millions embrace a noble position of atheism out of a sense of intellectual, spiritual, and moral integrity. I myself am an atheist about that particular concept of God.

Instead of keeping my definitions narrow or relying on one ideology, in this book I lean on a diverse constellation of scholars, poets, and other thinkers. I draw on wisdom from such ancients as Lao-tzu, the Sufi poets, the great prophets of Hebrew scriptures, the Buddha, as well as Jesus. I have also been guided in my spiritual journey by such modern-day thought leaders as Gandhi, Thomas Merton, Martin Luther King Jr., and Archbishop Desmond Tutu. Despite our varying and unique conceptual frameworks, we all regard the experience of the Beloved as deeper than any religious identity or division. Here, I am seeking to describe the universal dynamic that runs through every tribe, sect, and ideology. A core issue of life is negotiating the forces of fear and the forces of love within our own being and relationships. As each of us gains awareness of the power of love—the Beloved—working inside us to dethrone fear and open our hearts and minds, matters of religion and theology take care of themselves.

Embracing the Habits

There's a man I know named Don, an attractive, stocky accountant with jet-black hair and a timid smile. Ten years ago when he first arrived at All Saints Church in Pasadena, where I have been the rector for 17 years, he was contentious, skeptical, and tentative. He had been through a long and acrimonious divorce from his first wife, Sara, and he could not shake his feelings of rage and disappointment. Custody arguments kept him away from his firstborn son more than he desired. "I was paralyzed with the fear of the unknown, and I found solace dwelling in the resentment and regret of my former life," Don said.

Eventually, he met another accountant named Angela, whom he adored. Though he was somewhat anxious about remarrying, he loved and trusted Angela and wanted to build a new life with her. They married at All Saints and had a child together, joining Angela's young daughter from a previous marriage. Yet Don still felt lonely and unmoored. Late at night when he couldn't sleep, he lay in bed wondering how everything had gone so wrong. His accounting practice was financially successful, and he had a loving wife and beautiful, healthy children—surely he should be happy. But he was not. Something foundational was not working in his life.

During this time, Don was attending All Saints with Angela each week. In my Sunday sermons, I often talk about the Habits of Love, and I always emphasize the immense, liberating power we feel when we are able to open our hearts and our minds to love.

Don was listening. He heard the call of the Beloved, and he responded.

First, he worked at opening his heart to being more generous, so he could return to feeling a genuine and liberating sense of appreciation. "It takes hard work not to be drawn into what paralyzes us or makes us forget why we should be grateful. It is in gratitude for what we already have that we are reminded that we are beloved," Don said. His life is a busy one (as so many of ours are, too), full of responsibilities and activities, but he found ways to incorporate Stillness into his daily routine. Over time, he made a conscious effort to change the way he managed his relationship with Sara and their son. He tried always to choose love over fear. Instead of only talking about logistics with his ex-wife, he would ask Sara how she was doing—and when she answered, he listened. The anger in his heart began to dissipate. He tried to approach her with an intentional attitude of love.

"More and more, I opened my heart and myself to the possibility of love," Don explained. "Angela and I found ourselves hopeful and emboldened. The fear retreated." He also looked inside himself and saw where he had been giving too much of his energy over to fear. Knowing that it was now within his power to make different choices, he found peace with those choices he had made in the past: he forgave Sara, and he forgave himself. Joy began to seep into his life again. When he spent time with his children, he was often infused with a child-like spirit that allowed him to enjoy their company in a new and enriched way. And most important, through that process he began to recognize the Beloved in himself and in his first wife again. He released his fear and embraced the love within. Over time, Sara, seeing the change in Don's stance toward her, began to respond in kind.

Don credits this transformation to the work we do at All Saints of incorporating the Habits of Love into our lives. Naturally, the family dynamics are still complex and evolving, with daily challenges that each person tries to address with love rather than fear. Don emphasizes that his difficulties are not totally in the past. "Angela and I struggle daily to live in love with our former partners, and I don't want to suggest that it is perfect." As with all families, their lives are a work in progress, yet Don and his family's burdens have been lessened through their sincere and ongoing efforts to open their hearts.

And there's been another significant benefit too: in choosing to live in the consciousness of love, Don has not only improved his life but also, in incremental and meaningful ways, the lives of his family, colleagues, friends, and neighbors. His fresh outlook on life is stealthily and steadily transferred to everyone he comes into contact with, just as the beam of love in the picture hanging in my childhood bedroom transferred to me an all-pervasive sense of love and belonging. Without even realizing it, Don has taken his own important steps on the journey toward making our world a more harmonious place.

Open Your Hearts and Your Minds

If we can access the inner sanctuary living inside us and be brave on behalf of freedom, be brave on behalf of emotional, physical, relational, and spiritual health, be brave on behalf of unearthing the Beloved in every one of us—*then* we will know what we are called upon to do. The key to life, I think, and the most beautiful thing in the world is to know who we really are. We begin this journey by recognizing that we are deeply loved. We can live with an open heart and an open mind; we can be instruments of peace, reconciliation, and justice.

In preaching about the Habits of Love, I have had the honor of learning how everyday people gain joy and freedom from choosing love over fear—and now I seek to share those lessons with you. Living with love and methodically embracing its habits have changed many lives for the better. The Habits of Love helped Kathy find common ground with a friend from whom she had been distanced for many years. "I began to see her differently—to recognize her sincerity and her passion, although so different in direction from mine, was nonetheless rooted in a desire for good. Our relationship began to slowly change," she said.

Jerry and his brother Tod had not talked in many years, and when their mother was diagnosed with Alzheimer's disease, he considered not even sharing the news with Tod. But instead, Jerry chose to embrace love over fear and reach out, warmly and without bitterness, to his brother. Tod reconnected with his dying mother, and they began getting together weekly to engage in what they lovingly called "Swing Therapy" by making music together. "My mom was so filled with joy at the end of her life because our family was so close," Jerry explained. "And the best part of all is that my brother is now my very best friend."

When Carla attended her son's wedding, she had to deal with panic about having to face her ex-husband's new girlfriend for the very first time. Pulling over for a moment of Stillness in a parking lot before facing the crowd, she remembered that she was loved, and in so doing her fear retreated. "I felt comfortable enough to honestly smile and extend my hand, and realized that she too must have felt uncomfortable at that moment," Carla said. "I enjoyed everything about that beautiful evening, especially because—even though I was willing to fake it—in trusting love, no faking was necessary!"

Over the years, Adam has introduced the terminology of the loved and loving self versus the fearful self into his home. "An awareness of fear as love's opposite gives my wife and me, and our children, greater understanding of why people turn on one another, why exclusion, violence, and hate are so prevalent in our world," Adam told me recently. "Everyone knows fear, and if we believe fear is at the root of much misery, we can and should pledge to do our part to help dissolve that fear."

On a daily basis, practicing the habits expressed in this book will help you live a life grounded in the energy of this love. It isn't enough to know these things intellectually or to put them into practice sporadically. What is needed is experiential, trial-and-error practice. These are habits designed to help us forswear the reactive and fear-based thinking that causes us to make destructive choices—and leads us to avoid making important, transformative changes in our lives. As you will see, I came quite close to missing my own calling in life, and only by implementing the Habits of Love was I able to shift my perspective and find the courage to make the changes I so desperately needed. After that crucial turning point, I learned that such is the pattern of life: in every moment, some element of our loving self is at stake.

In my line of work, I hear from people with wildly divergent beliefs and from wildly varied places. I hear from those who struggle with personal fear and with abuse from religious and cultural practices. I hear from Christians of all stripes, as well as Jews, Muslims, Buddhists, the nonreligious, and even atheists about how inspired and hopeful they become when they hear the message of the Beloved. There is an enormous hunger and need in the world for spiritual guidance in living a life grounded in love and free of fear.

It is this hunger and the power these habits have to change lives that have convinced me it's time to get this message out. I hear a call to action, and I turn to you and call you to action too. Open your heart and you will be amazed at the transformations taking place all around you.

Come, my friend—will you join me on this adventure?

8 HABITS *of* LOVE

CHAPTER ONE

The Habit of Generosity

While on the shop and street I gazed
My body of a sudden blazed;
And twenty minutes more or less
It seemed, so great my happiness,
That I was blessèd and could bless.

—W. B. Yeats, "Vacillation"

The mighty Jordan River meanders along the eastern border of Israel/Palestine, giving life to two bodies of water, the Sea of Galilee and the Dead Sea. The Sea of Galilee teems with this life. Everywhere you look there is vitality. On the water, people are fishing, boating, and waterskiing; on the banks, people are relaxing, eating, and drinking. Everyone is enjoying themselves. Sixty-five miles to the south lies the Dead Sea. It is just that, dead. The reason for this stark contrast is simple: the Jordan River flows both into and out of the beautiful and vibrant Sea of Galilee. Inflow and outflow. Inhale and exhale. Receiving and giving, like our relationship with the Beloved. From the southern banks of the Sea of Galilee the river makes its way into the Dead Sea, but there the river stops. There is no outflow from the Dead Sea.

The human spirit, just like the seas, needs both inflow and outflow in order to foster life and create energy. When love flows out from within us, more flows in. When we open our hearts to love, we not only spread that love to others but also open ourselves to receiving love from others. Our outflow determines our inflow. The more we give, the more vital our lives, the bigger our spirits, and the deeper our living. When people are on the receiving end of Generosity, it opens their hearts in a way that is deeply transformative and sends ripples of love outward into the universe.

There was a critical turning point in my life when I experienced the power of Generosity just when I needed it the most. My father was an imposing man, barrel-chested with a sonorous voice and the capacity to steamroll others with whom he did not agree. For many years, I was a source of confusion and pain for him as he attempted to understand why I made certain decisions. In many ways, we were a mystery to each other, and as he lay in his bed at home in Georgia, preparing to draw his last breath, there was still much between us that had not been resolved.

I had been invited to become dean of a historic southern cathedral tested in the fires of the civil rights movement in Mississippi, where the community of believers was theologically and politically progressive as well as spiritually diverse and inclusive. The entire portrait of broad opportunities for transformational social action and service—as well as personal and professional development—made my heart beat fast with excitement.

Yet taking the job would mean uprooting my wife from her important work, displacing our children from their friends and school, and moving away from my home state of Georgia, where my loving family had lived for many generations. It would mean embracing my doubts and accepting the call to change in order that I might grow and help others do the same.

As soon as I was offered the job, I developed excruciating pain in my chest that left me short of breath. I felt as if my soul were pinned by the rubble of a fallen building. Was this a huge mistake? Would my family hold it against me? During this period of terrible indecision and angst, I flew to Bethesda, Maryland, to attend a seminar

with a new mentor, Dr. Ed Friedman. Like me, he was a practicing congregational minister. He was a rabbi; I, a priest. Like me, he
knew that the world of religion and the world of psychotherapy in-
tersected in dynamic ways.

I volunteered to present my dilemma as a case for Rabbi
Friedman and our group to address. With all the other students
looking on, he asked me question after question about my family—
not my nuclear family, but my family of origin. I found this startling.

I was the firstborn in a family of Southern Baptist clergy, I said.
My father, brother, and I had all been ordained Baptist preachers
in the rural southeastern corner of Georgia, described as "Christ
haunted" by novelist Flannery O'Connor. I talked for a long time
about my father, who had been a preacher, school principal, and
the superintendent of the public school system.

After a while, Rabbi Friedman looked into my eyes and said, "You
have to go to your father. You are about to strike out free from the
course he charted for you years ago. This move will most likely ensure that you will not return to the religious life, the area of the
country, and the culture in which you were raised. You have to go
directly to your father and ask him if that is all right with him."

Though I had made plenty of decisions that contradicted my father's own values, such as leaving the Baptist fold to become an
Episcopalian, the rabbi helped me see that I never had had the
courage to ask my father how he felt about what I was doing or to
explain to him what compelled me to make these choices. We just
didn't talk about it. On one level, our hearts and minds were closed
to each other. We were afraid of what might happen if we bared our
souls to each other. I realized that the panic I was suffering was anxiety about my father's disapproval. This realization stunned me. At
the lunch break after my presentation, I went straight to my hotel
room, called my home in south Georgia, and asked to speak to Dad.

I was trembling and pacing and sweating. He was so ill I could
barely hear him, and I did most of the talking. Becoming the Cathedral dean seemed the way I was supposed to go with my life, I

explained. Taking this job would mean that becoming an Episcopal priest was proving to be the right thing for me spiritually because it reflected my own authentic values. It meant that I would not be returning to Georgia where my family had lived for generations.

Then I sank onto the hotel room bed with my heart still racing and asked in a shaking voice, "Dad, all of this is very different from what you always had in mind for me. I need to know if all of this is okay with you."

I could sense my father summoning as much life force as he possibly could as he lay dying in the bed he had shared with my mother for 43 years. Finally, I heard him say, "Son, go for it."

Instantly, the chest pains I had been enduring disappeared. My trembling stopped. My voice returned. My father's words were the passport that took me from the constrictions of fear to the vast force field of love. By opening his heart and allowing the flow of love to run unimpeded into me—just as the Jordan River runs into and nourishes the Sea of Galilee—he gave me the strength I needed so I could release all the power of my own love into the world.

An Open and Generous Heart

Every human being is wired to be loving, accepting, compassionate, forgiving, caring, playful, courageous, and imaginative. But life often gets in the way. We hit roadblocks. We shut down and respond anxiously. Chronic fear overshadows each of our more loving human traits, making us reactive and closed minded while doing enormous damage to our physical selves. Science tells us that fear serves us well when there is a real threat to our existence. When we feel fear, blood automatically leaves the part of our brain that thinks, creates, and makes free choices and floods the part of our brain that makes automatic fight-or-flight decisions. In everyday life, however—life at home, at work, in the streets we walk daily—this fear-induced instinct does not serve us well.

There is a deep inner sanctuary in every one of us where this fear cannot set up headquarters. This inner sanctuary is where the Beloved dwells. When we connect with this sacred spot by opening our hearts, the walls imprisoning us evaporate. When we use the 8 Habits of Love to become aware of this sanctuary and to access its love, we become free to live fully as our authentic, loving selves. Fear's propensity to drive our lives is dispelled. We are liberated to tap into our capacity for imagination, creativity, care, healing, empowerment, and courage. And the most wonderful news of all is that every human being can "grow" the power of that inner sanctuary— the presence of the Beloved within—by making a practice of these habits until they become literally habitual.

A few months after our conversation, my father died. Though in his dealings with me, his wayward son, his loving self had sometimes been overshadowed by his fearful self, he knew as he lay on his deathbed that this was his final opportunity to show me heartfelt Generosity and thereby set me free. When my father opened his heart to me, extending the generative and loving gift of Generosity to me, he forever changed my life. I now remember my father as the man who told me to "go for it" so I could reach my greatest authentic potential. If this hadn't happened, the shame or doubt that came from wondering about his disapproval would have haunted me always. I might not have become Cathedral dean, which turned out to be a life-changing opportunity, revealing new dimensions in my life's work, service, and capacity. I was on the receiving end of his gift of self, and as a result I experienced an inner emancipation from many fear-based constraints to the loving flow of life.

Generosity comes from knowing that love is not a zero-sum game. The energy of love, of approaching life from your loving self, knows no limits. Whenever someone loves, more love is generated. Life flows. Imaginative ideas multiply. Cooperation and goodwill spread. Creativity-limiting fear diminishes. When people act from their fearful selves, not trusting that there is enough love and goodwill to go around, they not only hurt those in need but they hurt themselves too. They become like the Dead Sea, stagnant.

When we shrug off our negativity and insecurity, no longer covet and compete for what others have, and open our hearts to the dreams and values of others, we dwell in the spirit of Generosity. This enables us to approach the world from a loving, tolerant, open-minded place, which in turn infuses our interactions with energy that flows in both directions. Yes, Generosity means giving of our time, resources, and life force, but it also means giving people the benefit of the doubt, being able and willing to see the world from another's perspective, and loosening the tight grip we keep on ourselves. It is about blessing others with our thoughts and deeds. These blessings flow back to us in myriad ways.

Indeed, "to flow" is at the root of the word *affluent* (*affluere*). In the context of the Habit of Generosity, affluence is anything that flows toward others and is represented by our Generosity with whatever might be at our disposal—whether it is our attention, our material resources, or our care. If we see affluence as only meaning material wealth, then we may miss that *everyone* has the capacity to be affluent spiritually.

The Universe Is Kind

I once experienced something a student of mine called a "cosmic click." As a guest host for *Oprah's Soul Series* radio show, I was sitting in front of a vast sound mixer in a Chicago recording studio. Winter winds howled outside as I prepared to interview a man I greatly admired. I had long wanted to have an in-depth conversation with Stephen Mitchell since reading his translations of some of the world's most significant wisdom literature: the book of Job, the *Tao-te ching*, the sayings of Jesus, and the *Epic of Gilgamesh*. (These are among the oldest pieces of literature in existence—Mitchell would later tell me that all the works he has translated have the common thread of explaining how the universe works.) Now Mitchell was sitting opposite me. With earphones for both of us in place and the microphones adjusted, I asked this man, this poet, scholar, and translator, to recount how he found his way to his life work.

He told me a story about a devastating romantic breakup in his twenties. The pain in his heart was so great that he didn't know how to deal with it. A friend suggested he go to see a Korean monk, Seung Sahn, the great master of Zen Buddhism, who was working in the United States as an appliance repairman in Providence, Rhode Island. Mitchell arrived on his doorstep, intending to practice with him for a week or two; he stayed with him for four years.

It was clear to me in that Chicago radio studio that Mitchell had invoked one of the most sacred and defining moments of his life. The tone of our voices involuntarily shifted. The energy in the studio changed. We were in holy territory. He described practicing intensive meditation with the monk and experiencing transformations that would change the course of his life.

"What was the most important thing you learned while being with Seung Sahn?" I asked.

He did not hesitate. *"I learned that the universe is kind."*

Dead space on the radio is a cardinal sin. As the seconds ticked by, everything in the cosmos seemed to line up and make sense: I experienced a cosmic click. But despite my wishes, the large digital clock hanging on the wall in front of me signaled that it was time to end the show.

I calmly gave the appropriate sign-off, but my mind was spinning. I was reminded once again of the old push and pull of fear that had been instilled in me by a religion that sought to keep its flock in line through fear, as many religions do. Mitchell's benevolent view of the world contradicted the way I, and so many others, had been raised—to be fearfully vigilant about what the world could do to us. Some interpret the Bible to say that the world is "fallen" and "discontinuous" from the divinity of God. The narrative of "original sin" holds that something within us human beings and in the universe is corrupted. The continuity between the *Creator*—what we are calling the Beloved here—and the *created* has been severed. Our fallen-ness has destroyed the divine within. "There is no good within us," goes one of the prayers from the Anglican tradition. If this is so, then it surely can't be true that the universe is kind. But Mitchell's words refuted that prayer's claim, along with original sin's description of human existence.

Many people will look at their own lives and at the state of the world and harbor corrosive doubts as to whether this assertion about a fundamental, all-pervasive kindness can possibly be true. After all, we experience earthquakes, floods, tsunamis, fires, wars, oppression, terrorism, crime, injustice. Daily, people are evicted from their houses, the very heart and hearth of the family. They can't find employment. They are afraid of illness, job loss, and heartbreak. Around each corner lurks the next catastrophe. How, in the face of these realities, can we claim that the universe is kind? This is the perspective of the fearful self, the closed heart, and it is devastating.

This loop of fear causes us to remain blind to our own Beloved nature and the Beloved nature of others. It blocks us from seeing how effectively we can alleviate suffering in the world when we access our Beloved nature in order to work cooperatively for the common good. Even though the Beloved is inexhaustible, we become preoccupied by the fear of not having enough.

Because of the sometimes bitter realities of our political and economic environment, countless people are trapped in this fearful worldview. They are distrustful; perhaps they are disappointed in their families, their community, their leaders, and their religion. Their minds close. Albert Einstein once said that the most fundamental question we can ask ourselves is whether or not the universe is friendly or hostile. He suggested that the way you answer this question would determine your destiny. In the studio that day, I once again felt the call to let those people know the truth of Mitchell's words, and realize for themselves the immense release and freedom from fear they could enjoy if they accept and perpetuate this love-based view of the universe.

Communicating Kinship

My journey to becoming a priest has naturally involved officiating at a number of funerals. One beloved parishioner of mine, Sylvia, battled lymphoma for three years. Though she fought valiantly and with great determination, she left us too soon. During her funeral, I stepped aside and beckoned to her younger sister, Lisa, to come to the podium to give the eulogy, as Sylvia had wanted. Willowy and ashen, Lisa approached, her brow deeply furrowed. An accomplished businesswoman, she was accustomed to giving speeches to huge crowds in echoing conference rooms, but in church that day she appeared diminished and fearful. Just a few seconds into her remembrances, she stopped short. She could no longer speak. Sadness stole her breath. Tears ran down her face and her narrow shoulders heaved. No one among the five hundred gathered in the church exhaled. That room has never been more still.

After a moment, Sylvia and Lisa's 82-year-old mother rose, slipped out of her front pew seat, and with astonishing poise walked toward her only surviving offspring. Something unprecedented then took place. Rather than say anything to her weeping daughter, she simply stood right behind her. This mother became one of those slender but strong stakes placed beside a tomato plant to prevent it from breaking from the burden that bends it. Next, the mother's ever-so-slight bodily contact with her daughter's back began wordlessly but perceptibly to transmit composure into her daughter's body. There is a phenomenon in many religious traditions called "transmission," when the spirit and teaching of a master is imparted to a student or disciple. I observed this lady's daughter actually receive into her body the energy of her mother's equanimity and serenity. She found her missing voice. She returned to her text. Lisa was able to give an eloquent testimony to the beauty and grace of her deceased sister.

The congregation breathed, relaxed, and was as transformed as Lisa was. The eulogy came to its end. Mother and daughter, hand in hand, walked past the oak coffin, touched it lovingly, and returned to the pew of mourners. No embrace, eye contact, histrionics, or any other expression that might in any way distract from the miraculous transfiguration we had just beheld: a mother's stepping beyond her own grief in order to bestow, unselfishly and generously, the gift of life itself upon the next generation.

When someone literally has your back, love generously confers fortifying energy that casts out fear. Sylvia's mother provided a stirring example at Sylvia's funeral. Naturally entitled to all the grief in the world—one of the most difficult situations imaginable is the burial of one's son or daughter—this mother, while in no way denying her own grief, both acknowledged it and then gave of herself and her resources to her other child. Generosity is especially powerful when bestowed, as in this case, on a member of a younger generation by a member of the older generation (the word *generation* is directly related to Generosity). This is the life-altering gift my father had given to me before he died.

One way of looking at this habit is to understand that every act of Generosity is, in effect, giving a blessing. When one person blesses another, a certain power is unleashed. That power penetrates and outflanks all resistance arising from fear. Nothing may be apparent immediately from the outside, but the inner makeup of the individual who has been blessed has been touched; an alteration has begun, as with Lisa during her eulogy. As the Irish poet and Catholic scholar John O'Donohue noted, "When the gift or need of the individual coincides with the incoming force of the blessing, great change can begin." In his book *To Bless the Space Between Us*, he writes, "The world can be harsh and negative, but if we remain generous and patient, kindness inevitably reveals itself. Something deep in the human soul seems to depend on the presence of kindness."

A heartfelt and generous blessing does not, of course, require "blessing language"; it is connected to our own spirit—our loved and loving self—rather than to any specific religious practice. One morning I woke up to find an email in which the sender included this closing salutation: *Blessings Always.* The act of reading those words did indeed make me feel blessed. Blessings come in many forms—it can be the silent, unpreoccupied presence of another, a generous financial contribution, or a willingness to show patience or deflect the spotlight momentarily. I once received a well-timed blessing in a text message that said simply, "I think it's good being Ed." A friend, Hannah, makes a point of complimenting one person every day, whether it is a stranger in the street or a friend at the office. She will tell a woman in the corner store that her shoes are wonderful or comment favorably to a man on the train about the book he is reading. Seeing the surprise on their faces, watching the transformation as the recipient acknowledges and absorbs the blessing, is infinitely rewarding.

So we see that the Habit of Generosity is often as much about giving emotional or spiritual support as it is about giving money. At its core, it is about communicating kinship with others. In that somber, silent church, Sylvia's mother taught me—without using any words—the life-giving capacity the Habit of Generosity has to free someone from the grip of fear. The father who allows his irate six-year-old the time to collect himself before meting out punishment for a misdeed is showing Generosity. He is giving his child the gift of time and showing him that a rush to judgment is not only unnecessary, but can also be harmful. The young woman who rises from her seat in the bus to allow an elderly gentleman to sit down is behaving with Generosity by showing respect and declining to put her comfort first. Equally, adult children who support an ill parent by carving time from their hectic days to visit and sit in peace together are being generous by giving back to the universe that blessed them.

I have learned that we are most ourselves when, whether in everyday situations or when we face the most challenging of conditions, we can let our energy flow generously and unselfishly to another.

The Myth of Scarcity

My friend Alton is a millionaire many times over. But it was through him that I was reminded of how the fear of scarcity can make it challenging for even the most affluent among us to be generous rather than simply charitable. One December, Alton approached me at a holiday party that he and his wife were hosting. A large group of guests was standing in the dining room, sipping champagne from fluted crystal under the watchful eyes of two vibrant oil paintings of his forefathers, when he told us a story. Two days earlier he had gone to the bank and withdrawn $500 in ten-dollar bills from his account. He then jumped in his BMW and drove to the part of town where homeless people slept in the alleyways and under the weeping willows at the park. Feeling expansive, he handed out a ten-dollar bill to each of "the poor people."

"Ed," he said, gesturing toward me, "it felt so good to make those smiles come onto those faces of the downtrodden."

I bit my tongue as a way of trying to stay in the spirit of hospitality, but I promised myself I would have a conversation with Alton later. While he believed he was engaging the Habit of Generosity, he was actually revealing a deep-seated fear of scarcity that was holding him back from true Generosity. Generosity is not charity. Giving in the spirit of charity is self-referential: donations are seen as "coming from me and/or mine." Volunteer service becomes piety, of which one feels proud, as Alton did that night in his candlelit home. Actions motivated in this way conceal a meanness about whether or not the recipient is deserving. They also prevent us from engaging in such a way that people can help themselves— because the giving is more about *us* (and our "generosity") than it is about *them*.

The following October, during the annual stewardship season when we were asking everyone to make a financial commitment to the mission and ministry of the church, I decided to pay a call on Alton in his office at the end of the workday. After drinking some tea and making friendly small talk, I recalled his afternoon of charity to those who were homeless. I explained gently but in clear terms that increasing his giving to the church could have a more lasting effect on those who are homeless. A portion of all monies given to the church supports a center that gets the homeless into a program where they receive not only a bed to sleep in and food to eat, but also social service counseling in the interest of their becoming self-sufficient. The goal is to give those who are needy the tools to help themselves.

"Alton," I said, "I would like to invite you to give 10 percent of your annual income to your church."

"Oh, Ed, I can't give away 10 percent!" he said immediately. Then he offered a litany of reasons as to why this was impossible. The bottom line was that there wouldn't be enough for his family. "I tell you what I'll do, Ed. I'll ask my financial planner to tell me what I'm allowed to deduct from my income this coming year and I'll give you that. How does that sound?"

I soon received a pledge from Alton for $1,000—an increase of $250 over what he had given the year before. Preachers of all faiths can come under suspicion when they request giving to their church or temple, but I don't think it's a stretch to consider that a millionaire did not actually feel the power of Generosity with a gift that amounted to less than 0.01 percent of his net worth. Through these conversations, I saw how his relationship to his money was charity oriented. Making donations—whether of money or time—can be an act of power over others, rather than an act confirming that in reality we are in this boat of life together.

I don't mean to make this a discussion that revolves only around the idea of how generously we do or do not give away our hard-earned money. Rather, I am using this example to show that, in the specific case of the Habit of Generosity, we often worry about *not having enough*, financially or emotionally. This feeling flows directly from the force field of fear. I must hoard. I must grasp. I simply do not have enough to give even a little bit away: not enough money, energy, or forgiveness. I am depleted. This notion is especially prevalent in our culture today, given the fragile state of the world economy and of our precious Earth. But when we embrace the notion that at its core the universe is kind, we open ourselves to engaging in a generous inflow and outflow of energy from which, ultimately, everyone benefits.

Despite having great material wealth, Alton suffered from a mentality of scarcity in which he believed that the more he gave to others, the less he would have for himself and his family. It is often challenging for people to practice Generosity because they are hampered by the notion that they need more for themselves—whether it is more money, more acclaim, more attention, more patience, or more love. They see their capacities as finite. In some ways this is, of course, true—but in some ways it is patently untrue.

Growing up in Georgia, I knew a couple named Hardingale who lived in town. Mrs. Hardingale gave birth to four boys in quick succession, and it seemed their family was complete. Their modest three-bedroom, one-bathroom bungalow could barely contain them all, especially once the older boys hit their teen years. Sonya was a local schoolteacher, and John was a plumber. When their youngest son reached the age of ten, they began turning up everywhere—in the grocery store, at the gas station, in the dusty playground—with a fragile two-year-old girl they had adopted. She had pale skin and a wild head of black curls, and could barely bring herself to meet the gaze of anyone other than her new family.

For years Sonya, John, and the four boys had been volunteering each weekend at a shelter in the neighboring town: they cooked and cleaned, and the boys fixed things and played with the other children to help pass the quiet afternoons. Moved by the little girl's crippling shyness, and courageous despite their lack of means,

Sonya and John took Leah in when her mother could no longer take care of her.

"Life has been so generous to us," Sonya explained. "We have our health, our boys. Our house is filled with love. We have so much to give." Naturally, this family had less resources to expend on their older boys once they brought Leah into their family, but they also had more love to give. This in turn blessed their boys in a way that would impact them for the rest of their lives. They were not limited by the fear of scarcity.

The More We Give, the More We Receive

Generosity invites us to focus on something larger than ourselves. Once we choose to embrace Generosity, even though it may not initially seem natural, we open ourselves to receive from others. In every instance that I have been aware of someone exhibiting the Habit of Generosity, I have observed this act of "stepping over" our preoccupation with self or our internal resistance to give.

A friend told me of a couple she recently visited, Liam and Karen, who had had their first baby three weeks earlier. It was a boy: a nut-brown infant with milky, unfocused eyes and an impressive set of lungs. The family was living in a cramped, overheated rental, struggling through each day with little sleep and no downtime. There were plenty of hands to hold and soothe the baby, as Liam was out of work and Karen was on maternity leave. But the couple seemed to irritate each other with every little gesture they made, and as my friend was leaving she worried about how to advise them.

In the car on the way to the airport, she turned to Liam and smiled. "You're doing great," she said. "Just remember to be generous with each other."

She sensed that what these new parents needed, more than sleep or extra help, was an attitude *toward each other* of Generosity—

of patience, flexibility, and the willingness to give in and change if the moment called for it. The Habit of Generosity encourages another person's development rather than insisting that everyone else's thoughts, struggles, and challenges are really all about *you*. Wrapped up in their own individual experiences, Liam and Karen could not step outside themselves to see things from the other's perspective. Of course, once they begin being generous with each other regularly, they will find themselves on the receiving end of that Generosity too: what goes around comes around.

Too often we fear diluting our own power by giving some of it away to others. We fail to recognize that the very opposite is true. Our power increases rather than decreases when we share it. Karl is a manufacturing specialist who writes reports that influence the decisions big businesses make about which software to purchase. Though he is a leader in his organization, he often shares a byline with less influential co-workers. Rather than coveting the limelight for himself, he shares the wealth because he understands this will only strengthen his ideas, his message, and, ultimately, the benefits to his industry. Karl lives the maxim proposed by Mitchell that the universe is kind, and trusts that he will reap the benefits over the long run. Grateful for his own authority and influence at work, Karl seeks to share it with others and looks for nothing in return. As philanthropist Robert Woodruff, who made his millions at Coca-Cola, said, "There is no limit to what a man can do or where he can go if he doesn't mind who gets the credit."

I myself was reminded not long ago that the world is an infinitely better place when I do not behave as though it revolves solely around me. During my most recent annual retreat, I was staying at an elevation of 8,300 feet, near the headwaters of the Colorado River. Usually it takes people about 72 hours to acclimate at this altitude, but throughout the week I continued having terrific difficulties breathing and sleeping. As you can imagine, I was becoming chronically sleep deprived and felt I could not take even one deep, nourishing breath to sustain me. *Should I see a doctor?* I wondered.

THE HABIT OF GENEROSITY

My heart rate immediately shot up at the thought. I could not shake the idea that something was dreadfully wrong with me.

The nearest medical center was a twenty-minute drive away. Leaning heavily on the receptionist's desk, I had barely uttered the words "shortness of breath" when a booming voice rang out over the public address system calling for a triage nurse to come immediately. She bustled me off to an emergency room bed, placed an oxygen feed in my nostrils, drew blood, and took an EKG. My heart still racing uncomfortably, I tried to put a dozen worst-case scenarios out of my mind.

During a lull in the activity, after a nurse brought me a cup of cold water and I was the recipient of dozens of other kindnesses from the ER staff, the essence of the Habit of Generosity suddenly came to me. One particular nurse, Gale, with her head tilted in concentration and her clear, caring eyes assessing me, kept peppering me with questions about the nature of this book, *8 Habits of Love*, that I had mentioned I was working on. She wanted to know what the eight habits were. "How wonderful to have access to a book that could help me with my daily navigation through fear," she responded eagerly. She whipped out a pencil from the pocket of her uniform and wrote the title down, saying she would order it as soon as it was published.

This woke me from a slumber of self-absorption. It occurred to me that I was so focused on whether I was having a heart attack that I had not even considered I could at that moment also extend myself in the service of Generosity—even as a patient in the emergency room. I realized that I could be just as interested in her spiritual life as she was in mine. So I asked Gale about her spiritual interests. Somewhat bashfully, she described them to me and confessed that she had thought about writing a book detailing her own path as someone who cares about spirituality in the midst of her activity of nursing.

"You should definitely write that book," I said. "I'm certain it would help me—and many others too."

Gale turned to me with a smile that radiated a completely different energy than the professional smile she had been wearing. Though we still barely knew each other, our mutual Generosity had opened up the dam that allowed healing waters to flow between us. We established a trust and an intimacy that almost seemed tangible, as though the very air in the room had changed.

Over the next two hours something new emerged in that emergency room. One different kind of exchange led to another. No one had to label it "blessing" or "generosity" or "kindness." Laughter rose and fell. I could feel myself begin to unwind. Others seemed to be relaxing. By the time the doctor discharged me with a clean bill of health and the stern order to drink more water, my blood pressure had returned to normal—in itself a good sign—but I also left profoundly and gratefully moved.

The universe, as represented by all of the people who had come to my aid, was generous that day. As, I believe, it is every day.

The Struggle to Be Generous

No matter how good our intentions, there are situations in which being generous can present a seemingly insurmountable challenge. In each of the transformative stories in this chapter, the practitioner chose Generosity in the face of some internal resistance. This resistance is often erroneously considered a "natural" or "human" reaction. One of the most intriguing things about the appearance of Generosity is that despite a reflexive, internally erected barrier against being generous, there is also this quiet, sacred hunch that comes to individuals that the appropriate response to the abundant kindness and beauty in the universe is to share. Yet is it really possible to step outside yourself and recognize the needs of others, especially if you are already stretched thin or if the person or persons you are dealing with are ungrateful—or worse, rude and inflexible themselves?

Last year my friend Dan had an experience that called for Generosity when his instinct was to protectively cry, *no*! He had just become executive director of a Jewish Community Center in Philadelphia when the center's events coordinator was scheduled to take a sabbatical. At the same time, another colleague, Hattie, asked Dan if she could reduce her hours to work on an outside project she had been postponing for many years.

That night, Dan went home and developed a splitting headache. The timing was terrible. He was annoyed, almost angry, to find himself in such a weakened position just as he was supposed to be settling into his new job. Entrusted with the mission to turn the center around and bring it back into the black, he was now faced with the prospect of losing two key employees.

Once his initial sense of panic and frustration subsided, he began to see things from outside the perspective of his own immediate needs and wishes. Hattie had been at the center for almost six years. Dan knew she had put in many late nights at the office. The past week, she'd come to work looking very tired. It was obvious she was burned out. He could ask her to stay working full time over the summer, and he knew that she would. She was responsible and truly cared about the organization. But he knew in his heart that she needed this time off.

Was there any way to look at the good side of this situation? Could there be a benefit to his losing his two key employees just as he was figuring out how the center really functioned?

As he felt himself begin to relax—he was beginning to look at this from the perspective of his loving self—it occurred to Dan that he'd be saving significant money for the next eight weeks if he gave the go-ahead to both these people. What could he do with the extra money—already budgeted but no longer needed for their salaries? He could put it toward revamping the center's creaky old website. By the time his events coordinator and Hattie returned to work in early September, the new website would be up and running, drawing in new members each day. By allowing himself to disconnect from his fearful self and see his situation through a different lens, an opportunity had presented itself to him and his organization. He was able to be generous, and, in the long term, actually benefit from what had seemed to be a serious setback.

Being Open to Creative Problem Solving

But what if the balance of power does not tip in your favor? How often I hear from people who are trapped in a work environment that is toxic. Each day they head to the office with a pit in their stomachs—perhaps a co-worker is a bully, or the culture is too competitive, or the employees seem to be working against each other enviously. There is no spirit of Generosity at play. Susan works in a clinic in which the daily atmosphere is full of tension. She has two bosses in particular who define the destructive spirit of the place.

Over the past year, work has become so unbearable that she has considered quitting. But Susan has long-term patients to whom she is attached. The clinic is near her home, and she likes a number of her co-workers who are in a different department, with whom she eats lunch sometimes. As we will see later as we explore the remaining seven habits, Susan is not really trapped; there are ways she can access her Stillness, find her Truth, and convey this to her bosses with Candor in the spirit of Generosity. In the meantime, she practices Generosity by her willingness to make the best of a bad situation. She can't change the culture of the organization overnight, but she can change her attitude about it. As such, she launched a pub night once a month; initially only few people turned up. But after a few months, one of the bosses with whom she had clashed attended, and for the first time ever she was able to see him in an entirely different context. When she went to work the next day, things did not seem so unbearable. Her heart had opened. She began to look for opportunities to be generous at work, with her "enemies" as well as her friends, and over time the tension lessened.

As a teenager, I worked as a delivery boy for an auto parts store. Though trying my very best, I was often goofy and occasionally inept, a thorn in the side of my immediate manager, Bill. When I was late or forgot something, and especially when I delivered a part to the wrong address, Bill would get an earful from the store's manager. But there was no drama and *oh-look-what-you've-done!* Instead, he would take me aside, put his hefty arm around my shoulders, and explain where I had gone wrong. His Generosity in the face of his own manager's impatience and his ability to see the problems as something I was doing—rather than a negative reflection on my character—was a gift to me as a young man.

Though I learned a lot from Bill's Generosity, I would later come to realize that I myself was by no means immune to the struggles of acting with Generosity. About six months after our initial discussions about annual donations to the church, Alton decided to pull all his giving from All Saints. He didn't like a sermon I had preached. When I called him to discuss it, he gave me a piece of his mind, insisting this was not the church he had known before.

I decided to pay him another personal visit. This time I was scared, angry, and intimidated. I became quiet and still before going to see him and the idea came to me that I needed to extend to him the Generosity that I didn't experience his extending to the world. In the moment, I resisted the temptation to devise a strategy that would change Alton's mind, and instead I decided to simply be giving to him in every way possible. As soon as I made that decision all of my fear and self-absorption was replaced by a flow of life-giving energy. My visit to him became nothing more than an attempt to transmit the energy of kindness his way, no matter what he might say to me. It was not an instant miracle. However, as we sat there a different attitude gradually came over Alton. We talked about his health, his family, and his faith. We reestablished a tentative, tender strand of friendship that was unattached to any results.

I became aware of how my desire to change Alton had also been an act of charity in which I intended to dole out my values about

Generosity in conditional measurements. In my relationship with him I had believed in the power of Generosity and yet I had behaved condescendingly and ungenerously toward him. It was not until I extended kindness to him (better yet, let the kindness of the universe flow through me) that he and I could meet in a new emotional space: the space of Generosity.

However you choose to spread Generosity, remember especially that when you are faced with a challenge—a self-centered, rude, or closed-minded person for example—a Generosity-oriented response will always affect that challenge to some degree for the better. Though my relationship with Alton was never perfect, even when we disagreed we were able to find common ground when we approached each other with open hearts and open minds in the spirit of Generosity. That common ground forms the basis from which goodness can eventually flow outward.

The Blessings of Gratitude

Ingratitude is arguably the most destructive character trait of all. It destroys relationships and it destroys the human soul. "Blow, blow thou winter wind, / Thou art not so unkind / As man's ingratitude," wrote Shakespeare in As You Like It. Ingratitude ignores the fact that each one of us is a sea into which some confluence of springs, rivulets, and rivers have flowed. The only way we could have become who we are is through the flow into our lives of the energy of the Beloved and the Beloved's energy in other persons. Ingratitude says, "Everything I have I earned by my own hands; all of it came to me as a result of my own work." All the Habits of Love conspire to expose delusion and falsehood. The Habit of Generosity targets the lie of ingratitude.

For me, the knowledge that Generosity is rooted in a belief in abundance and a life of gratitude is embodied in the unsinkable spirit and springlike freshness of a woman named Elizabeth.

Elizabeth is a vital, intellectually curious businesswoman in her eighties. She is still going strong with no hint of retirement in the air. Her gleaming red Cadillac speaks volumes about her effervescence, her audacity, and her choosing the bright side of life as her focus. Every workday she goes to the office, oversees her investments, and stays in touch with the various organizations she supports—from church to theater to the California Institute of Technology. She loves learning about scientific frontiers, rarely turning down an opportunity to attend lectures about groundbreaking research. Elizabeth is a healer, whose hands have been conduits for healing energy for many. An early feminist, she helped lead All Saints to change the language used for worship to be more inclusive, and supported the ordination of women to the clergy.

Elizabeth is no stranger to heartbreak and great personal loss. Unscrupulous business partners have cheated her out of millions, one of her sons suffered a life-threatening illness as a child, and her beloved husband's mental and physical health are currently assaulted by Alzheimer's. Her acquaintance with grief brings her to tears. She has had thousands of opportunities to become a Dead Sea, yet she acknowledges her breaking heart and then moves forward. She consistently turns her back on fear and its designs for her to go through life in a stingy, overly protective way.

She quite happily recounts that her vibrancy stems directly from her life of Generosity. Elizabeth knows in her very being that the scarcity mentality is a delusion. Wherever there is divine energy, which she sees and experiences all around, there is an abundance of healing, love, and financial resources—and this only increases when you give it away. There is always more on its way. The Sea of Galilee pulls ever more water from its source.

"All giving is ultimately for the individual who is giving, more than for the institution to which you're making a donation," Elizabeth explained with confidence. "God and the universe want you to be healthy and wealthy. They need your willing participation in receiving that health and wealth, and the willing participation is measured by your helping others to be healthy and wealthy. Gratitude is a huge part of this. You simply cannot make your focus how bad things are in your own life and in the world and expect to be fully alive. It is important to focus on how wonderful things are and be grateful and generous." Elizabeth knows that her vitality is directly connected to her giving. She is not motivated by the idea of charity, but by the love that is in her soul that she chooses to share, much in the same way that the exhausted couple with the new baby will be giving abundantly as they show each other Generosity in stressful times when patience is hard to access.

Delight may take place in the heart of the recipient of Generosity, but it is the person who *exhibits* Generosity in spite of everything that is holding him or her back who experiences an inner reconfiguration.

How to Practice Generosity

Fear can lead us to live lives of self-absorption, in which we covet blessings instead of conferring them on others. We find we can't let go, we assume the worst, we feel insecure, we act without thinking—or perhaps we do not act enough. It is hardly surprising that amid the pressure of day-to-day life and under the yoke of a fearful culture many of us struggle to open our hearts and be generous.

But as the wise Stephen Mitchell reminded me on that winter day in Chicago, if we can only trust that ultimately the universe is kind, we will be released from the fear of scarcity that drives us. We will be able to live with gratitude and extend that gratitude outward in the service of others. Consciously practicing the Habit of Generosity will help us live our lives in the spirit of loving abundance.

Make a list of five things for which you are grateful today. You may have some previous experience with such a gratitude list; this time notice the change in yourself—in your energy field—as you write.

See if you can feel your fearful self actually shifting to your loving self. Notice that all of those items on your list were gifts to you from some other hand. Consider yourself as a Sea of Galilee with the joyful responsibility of sharing with others what you have received from others.

* Take an inventory of the relationships in which you are afraid. Has a co-worker consistently belittled you in the office? Is a parent disapproving of your life choices? Do you have a friend you have hurt or disappointed, or vice versa? Experiment with visiting one of these individuals—this can be in your mind initially, until the courage comes whenever possible and/or practical for you to see this person face to face. Before the visit, take some time to think in peace. Adopt an attitude that you are going merely to bless this person, to express the kindness of the universe to him or her. Notice how your fear subsides.

* The next time you are in a meeting—whether a formal meeting or sharing a meal with a friend—end with a moment in which everyone can express their appreciations and their regrets. At All Saints, we train every committee chair to end meetings this way; this is a chance to acknowledge the kind and generous acts of another, or to acknowledge our own failures to act in such a manner. Once sufficient space is given, which at first can seem quite uncomfortable, almost every time someone will have noticed a moment of kindness contained in another's remark or concern. That in turn gives rise to someone else mentioning another moment in the meeting that meant something to him or her. In short order the energy in the room has existentially changed. You may find you leave your meeting to deal with your next responsibilities with a different outlook. Each person becomes more aware of something sacred in the world and in life. You may never call it the Beloved, but you carry a different vibrational frequency out of that encounter.

* Consider how much money you currently give away every year. Compare it proportionally to your annual household income. Stretch yourself to give away a larger percentage; you could start with 10 percent of your spending money. Be aware of the effect that this giving has on your fear quotient. My experience is that with every percentage point I give approaching 10 percent of my *total* income and then beyond, the less clenched and fearful I am about money, and the more careful I am in budgeting the rest. Those of us throughout the world who give 10 percent or more know that the remaining 90 percent goes much farther as a result of having given the 10 percent away.

* Perhaps you are deeply in debt or your budget just barely meets your needs, and you find giving away money causes too much anxiety for you to do so with equanimity. But we all do have the capacity to give, even if it is only a little. Each small effort at financial Generosity brings you closer to leaving behind your fear of scarcity. Even when money is tight we have a tendency to buy lattes, grab a T-shirt that is on sale, rent a car we may not actually need. Work toward incrementally eliminating these small purchases and putting that money aside instead, for a cause that moves you. In this way, you are taking small but important steps toward shrugging off the sometimes crippling anxiety that has taken root in our modern society regarding money and material goods.

* Small kindnesses can have enormous impact on how others feel. Instead of limiting your outreach to special times of year like holidays or birthdays, reach out to family, friends, or even strangers randomly to let them know you are thinking of them and are sending love their way. It might be just a quick text or voice mail. It might be a card or the gift of a visit. Perhaps it is the gift of a smile; I am amazed at how my day changes when I smile and speak to strangers. First, their face almost always responds by mirroring my smile; they look like the person they *want* to look like—a person who is loved. Second, my own

day changes when realizing that strangers can be generous to one another and feel a kinship just by greeting one another with a smile. I believe this simple act also reduces the overall amount of stress in the world.

All of the remarkably generous, generative, affluent people I have ever known were profoundly grateful. Gratitude is the key to being affluent. Think of the people in your past or present to whom you are grateful. Perhaps it is the elementary school teacher who helped you conquer your fear of talking in front of the class. It could be your own child, who makes you laugh every day. It may be a spouse who is always in your corner, or a parent who nurtured and guided you— even when you were at your most difficult as a teenager. Let this lead you to think of creative ways you might give back to your community. You could attend a class at your local public school and give a talk about your career choice. You could donate supplies to a day care center. You could serve dinner at a battered women's shelter or visit the elderly at a retirement home. This allows the flow of kindness to continue unobstructed, in and out like healing waters, and contributes to the wellness of the universe. In the words of the German theologian Meister Eckhart, "If the only prayer you ever say in your entire life is thank you, it will be enough."

CHAPTER TWO

The Habit of Stillness

I know the way you can get
When you have not had a drink of Love:

Your face hardens,
Your sweet muscles cramp.
Children become concerned
About a strange look that appears in your eyes...

Squirrels and birds sense your sadness
And call an important conference in a tall tree.
They decide which secret code to chant
To help your mind and soul. . . .

I know the way you can get
If you have not had a drink from Love's Hands.

—Hafiz

When I was seven years old, my baby brother was born. This was a time of great joy and upheaval in our household, and I often found myself alone. One late morning, as the sun was beginning to scorch the blacktop and the insects buzzed noisily in the humid air, I entered a stand of pines next to my childhood home in Georgia—

the kind of stand seen in many large yards of the American South. Underneath my bare feet lay a thick blanket of soft pine needles. The aroma enveloped me, and I felt myself cushioned on all sides — by the softness of the needles and black earth beneath my feet, by the warm air pressing against my skin, but also by something new and intangible. I suddenly felt myself being embraced by what I now call the Beloved. At the time I did not know what it was.

I had been playing very actively in the yard, and was a little out of breath. As this intangible and wondrous feeling came over me, I stopped moving and became a receptacle for the experience. Standing in Stillness among the pines, my heart slowed down and I was very calm. The embrace I felt was like an inaudible voice, or a sudden *knowing*, an unexpected revelation all of my own. One instant I was a tousled, active young boy playing in a pine grove. The next, I was the most special, loved being in all creation. At the very same time I understood — as I had begun to suspect when I gazed upon the picture of the Revelation in my parents' Bible — that every other creature was the most special, loved being in all creation as well. I felt powerful and creative, full of energy and imagination. Nothing seemed too difficult — and I knew that every other person on the planet had been given equally special gifts.

Life comprises both ordinary and extraordinary moments when we need to imagine, dream, plan, strategize, and nurture ourselves and others. This is hard to achieve when we react to everyday life with anxiety. When we are full of fear, being open hearted becomes virtually impossible. We are stalled; we cannot grow or find imaginative solutions. Yet this habitual fear is not always easy for us to recognize — it takes on many masks. Frantic parents are acting from fear, for instance, when they see every failure, medical concern, or minor setback their child experiences as a life-or-death crisis rather than as an opportunity for development — but they would likely never characterize it as being fear based. Similarly, people who are stuck in relationships that aren't working don't always recognize that it is fear that is keeping them from facing their problems or making risky changes. In the workplace, colleagues who see unplanned developments or problems as a contemporary Armageddon fail to realize that reverting automatically to calamity mode holds them back from actually being able to solve their problem. Their creative problem-solving skills are impeded. Every person slips all too easily into the habit of fear.

Stillness is pivotal in overcoming the sometimes subtle but invariably destructive power that chronic fear has over us. Thomas Keating, a Trappist monk and prolific author, once said that our minds, hearts, and souls are like basins of silty water. When stirred, the water is cloudy and our vision obscured. But when the water has been at rest, the silt filters down to the bottom, leaving the water clear. We can then see our lives and our interactions with others with greater clarity. In this moment of Stillness among the pines, I experienced what it feels like to be connected with the Beloved, the source of the most powerful tool in our lives: *love*.

Warming Our Hearts

Stillness is as much a physical experience as it is a psychological and spiritual state. As the muscles in our bodies let go of their tension in Stillness, the inner condition of our body changes from being tense and overheated to being clean and refreshed. Our breathing transitions from choppy and irregular to a calm and slow rhythm.

With those physical changes come quietly powerful transformations. It is as if our minds are sinking below the surface waters of life where turmoil, confusion, and chaos reign. As we submerge into a cooling Stillness, all the disparate parts of ourselves come together at our core; they are, in effect, reunited with that part of our soul that cannot ever be disturbed because it is the dwelling place of love. It is our loving self, the Beloved within us.

Spiritual greats in the past have talked about their hearts being strangely warmed and feeling physically unclenched, but they also describe feeling energized. When love is being fully accessed, one is able to feel a profound mixture of peace and joy but also power. It is important to note that when we are accessing our core, we are still aware of anger or fear or sadness when they arise in ourselves and in others. It's just that the anger, fear, or sadness arise and are dealt with in the crucible of peace, joy, and power.

Here is an extraordinary reality: in any and all circumstances, we can become free from fear's grip by accessing that crucible of peace, joy, and power within. An important step toward becoming familiar with this inner sanctuary of love in ourselves and in others is through coming to Stillness.

The work of the contemplative activist and monk Thomas Merton has profoundly influenced me, and his words are enlightening. He wrote of this place of Stillness, "It is untouched by sin and by illusion, a point of pure truth, a point or spark which belongs entirely to God...which is inaccessible to the fantasies of our own mind or the brutalities of our own will or of anybody else...It is like a pure diamond blazing with the invisible light of heaven. It is in everybody." By allowing the murky waters of our lives to clear through practicing the Habit of Stillness, we can always gain access to this light-filled diamond—this inner strength that is always there to guide us and that nothing can ever destroy.

The Urgent Call to Stillness

All of us know on an abstract level that when we are caught in the frenzy of "normal life" in Western culture—and sadly, increasingly in Eastern cultures—it is difficult to make fruitful decisions. We cannot respond to unique situations with the imaginative and tuned-in behavior that they require. When fear drives us, our minds are less creative. Jonathan Franzen, the gifted twenty-first-century novelist, notes that Stillness is the "point where you can actually make responsible decisions, where you can actually engage productively with an otherwise scary and unmanageable world." That point of Stillness rings like a bell struck during meditation; it is pure and exquisite—and utterly precious.

Though we are constantly being admonished to "slow down" and "take it easy," it is among our greatest challenges to put into practice the Habit of Stillness. The great majority of us feel that our lives are already much too full—of activities, responsibilities, even possessions. We are told to exercise, to go to mosque, temple, or church, to practice meditation. We are told to put down our smartphones, not work on weekends, take time to think deeply, banish distractions.

Many people consider the idea of some form of meditation practice as the impractical activity of monastics or counter-culturists seeking to live off the grid. They simply don't believe that they have 20 or 30 minutes to give to something as "self-absorbed" as coming to Stillness. They are far too active and diligent. Too many people rely on them. The demands on their lives are too pressing.

Over the years, I have come to view reaching daily Stillness the way I view my morning shower and tooth brushing. I spend an hour each morning in Stillness—which, for me, is my deepest form of praying—and I don't want to enter my day without this act of spiritual, mental, and emotional hygiene. However, I don't always succeed in pulling off the Habit of Stillness.

On a memorable Friday, for example, when I hadn't arranged sufficient time to reach Stillness, I found myself unable to react to the circumstances of my day with any shred of creativity or Generosity. After a hurried breakfast, I got to my office and turned on my computer. In my inbox was an email marked URGENT from one of my parishioners. He had heard that the boss of a right-wing radio talk show host was on our Board of Governors. In his note he asked, "How could a church with our peace and justice agenda elevate to such a level someone whose behavior is so destructive to the health of the country?"

Reading those words, I felt attacked. I took his questions and implied criticism personally, and so I reacted with an attitude of defensiveness rather than Generosity. I wrote an email back that I soon came to regret. In fact, when I met with the parishioner some days later—when I had started the day with Stillness that grounded me in knowing and feeling myself and everyone else as Beloved—I understood perfectly that his intent had never been to challenge me personally or professionally. He had simply meant to raise the question as an item for discussion. I had read him with the wrong mind-set, in the spirit of fear and with a closed heart, and as a result had some unfair and resentful thoughts. I jumped to the conclusion that he was being judgmental, and so I fed that misperception by re-acting judgmentally myself. Without having accessed Stillness, my instinct had been toward defensiveness and dogma.

Dogmatic choices are made solely in reaction to a crisis at hand, a crisis most often presented by an anxious culture, an anxious per-son, or by our own anxious thoughts. When we are tired or frenzied and we do not stop for some form of Stillness—some form of prayer, meditation, reflection, rest, healthy diversion—we do harm to our-selves. Fear feeds on frenzy and fatigue.

In contrast, the Habit of Stillness, when practiced over time, transforms us as it connects us to our inner sanctuary every day, preventing us from reacting defensively in life and in relationships. With Stillness, we are open to life and are lovingly present.

Let me give you another example. On a day when I had enjoyed a powerful journey to Stillness, I received a call about the death of a famous person who was a personal friend of a church member. The family of the deceased wanted to know if All Saints would be willing to be the venue for his funeral just three days later. Such an elabo-rate event would involve security, news media, and a lot of work on our part.

As a consequence, rather than having time to write, reflect on, and prepare my sermon as I had planned, I spent four intense hours in my office with the bereaved family that afternoon. The great sur-prise to me during that long meeting was that I felt patient, warm, inviting, pastoral, and supportive rather than rushed, tense, and resentful—all hallmarks of fear. The family and I were nourished by a tender, enriching time together. I could find inside me no umbrage lurking under a veneer of professional politeness; instead, I was able to surrender to the serendipity of the day. My experience is that when I can inoculate the day with Stillness, I am constantly surprised by the gifts I find hidden within it.

Reaching God-Consciousness

Last year, after I heard that a preacher from Florida threatened to burn the Koran, I invited speakers to All Saints to tell us about the Koran. A dangerous swell of religious bigotry was growing in America—based in the fear of the unknown—that was encouraging us to hate an entire people and disavow an entire religion. Somehow, this hatred is supposed to make us feel "safer." This is fear-based, closed-minded thinking at its worst. A young woman named Aisha came to give a presentation at our church. Standing in front of a crowded room, dressed modestly, in keeping with Islamic practice, she seemed both self-assured and nervous at the same time. Tucking a wayward strand of hair behind one ear, she listened intently to our questions.

"What does reading the Koran mean to you?" I asked finally.

"Well," she said, pausing to think, "it means coming to God-consciousness."

For me, this is the essence of what we seek when we practice the Habit of Stillness, yet we all do it in our own unique way. A graduate school advisor once told me, "You can be exposed to the finest thinking available, but it won't do you or anyone else any good if you don't cook it on your own stove." In reaching Stillness, we are all seeking to come to God-consciousness in our own distinctive ways. Personally, I access Stillness through silent prayer, which could also be called meditation or contemplation.

Each morning when I am at home, I go to a particular chair I've been using for years. It is in a corner of the living room, where it is warm in the winter and cool in the summer. Sometimes it is as early as four or five a.m., and I wrap myself in a shawl made for me by a group in my parish who gather weekly to knit such "prayer shawls." Occasionally, even after five, ten, fifteen minutes, nothing happens. Concerns, suspicions, images of adversaries, and lists to remember mix together in a chaotic cocktail with dream fragments and mis-spoken words between my wife and me, or my colleagues and me.

This is a period I think of as pre-prayer: the silt is still swirling in the basin and has yet to settle. To be honest, sometimes I do not make it through this stage. On those days I stop after about 20 min-utes feeling rather unfulfilled and unsettled. Most days, however, an unfolding awareness tells me to stay put for a little longer and then a little longer still. The first signal that I am coming to Stillness is a relaxation inside my shoulders and upper arms that feels like the gradual unclenching of a fist. I know something is about to happen. The silt is falling to the bottom. My breathing begins to slow and deepen in response.

In the second phase of Stillness, the water in the basin appears to now be a beautiful blue color. The longer we remain with this sen-sation, the more the water becomes the very nature of our being; we are invited to enter it, and the water becomes our air. This is not just any air, but a kind of mentholated oxygen that is like moving from the air of a sweltering afternoon to that of a fresh Alpine morning. This period of time is profoundly restorative. My fears evaporate. I am loved and cared for. Everyone else is loved too. Everyone else is cared for. I rediscover the Beloved existing in the center of my true being, and when I have arrived there, I am home.

The transition to the next phase of Stillness shows us one of the true faces of the Beloved: the desire to pray for other people. On any given day, I know that my Stillness has progressed to its final phase when I mentally encounter both those on my prayer list as well as some surprising people I have not thought about in a while, or I have too often thought of in a resentful or angry way. Often I am stunned by this particular constellation of individuals. A community has been assembled into this sacred space by an energy beyond my control.

In this place, there is simply no room for fear. In 30 minutes or so, I have traveled from a swirl of my own fears and preoccupations and jitters to a relaxing of my muscles and whispered signals that Stillness is taking me to my deepest self. John O'Donohue, the Irish poet and scholar, calls this a place "where you have never been wounded, where there's still a sureness in you, where there's a seamlessness in you, and where there is a confidence and tranquility in you...the intention of prayer and spirituality and love is now and again to visit that inner kind of sanctuary."

Getting Your "Tutu On"

Coming to Stillness is a unique experience that can and must be tailored to suit unique individuals. My friend Jessica is a highly successful businesswoman in Washington, D.C., where she directs the communications department of a large U.S. federal agency. Unexpected challenges coming from every direction comprise her daily work agenda. But far from appearing strained and protective, Jessica effervescently engages everyone she meets. She has a ready smile and friendly eyes.

One evening in Southern California, where I now live, I was attending a street party given by a mutual friend. There was a brisk breeze and we all wore sweaters. The setting sun was a gloriously warm orange in the cool sky. Four musicians playing jazz on the street corner set the tone of beauty, joy, and celebration. That night Jessica introduced herself to me. She told me about the last time she'd been in Pasadena, when she had attended All Saints and heard Archbishop Desmond Tutu preaching.

"He changed my life," she said to me, her blue eyes blazing.

I knew the visit she was describing; it was one of the most powerful Archbishop Tutu had ever made to our church. I was jubilant. "In what way did he change your life?" I asked, leaning toward her. The wind and the music whistled lightly in my ears.

"I developed a habit as a result of that visit—now, whenever chaos erupts at work, I retreat to my office, close the door, and stay there until I 'get my Tutu on,'" she explained. "Everyone on my team knows that I'm not prancing around in a ballet outfit, but my secret expression means I've got to compose myself. They'll often say, 'Oh, Jessica, she's just getting her Tutu on.' It's become a great joke in the office."

"Oh boy," I said, laughing. "Getting your Tutu on?"

At its heart her story was about finding her own distinctive habit of coming to Stillness. When she feels stressed, she knows that her best self will emerge if she can recapture how she felt when she was in church with Archbishop Tutu.

"I remember feeling joy, love, and total acceptance," she said. "The archbishop gave me a kind of clarity in which I physically saw nothing, but I felt my deep personal truth coupled with the confidence to accept it." She then explained that only when she feels fully engaged with that reality—to the point that she can share that feeling with other people—does she feel she's got her Tutu on. Instead of spinning in chaos or frustration, the power of the Tutu brings her back to where she can be the leader she knows she is. In Stillness, she can reset her mind.

Jessica is a busy, responsible person—a problem solver who knows that she will waste valuable time when she addresses her tasks from a mind-set that is incapable of finding the most creative answers to her problems. She understands that Stillness has immense value for her. Albert Einstein made this point when he said that we cannot solve problems with the same consciousness that created the problem in the first place. I am convinced that we can create new solutions to the old problematic questions we face that arise from our culture and the machinations of fear. But the human brain, overdosing on fear, simply cannot access the faculties of imagination, compassion, or vision necessary to come into possession of those solutions without regularly accessing Stillness.

Finding a Rhythm

Many rituals that involve quiet activity, whether performed alone or with others, can be conduits for Stillness. Prayer and meditation provide consistent, tranquil outlets for the millions of people around the world who practice one of the world's religions. But for many, the opportunities for self-reflection and centering that are offered up by organized religion hold no appeal. Luckily, this is no impediment to finding Stillness. You may encounter Stillness while on your daily commute, while exercising, or while listening to music. You may find it outdoors or indoors, with a much-loved pet or in solitude. Each of us can experiment and find our unique practice of the Habit of Stillness, which is a foundational habit for opening your heart and your mind, allowing you to experience your loved and loving self and practice the other habits in this book.

When I was in my early thirties I suffered a profound depression. This happened around the time I left the church of my youth — the Baptist Church of my family of origin. I began attending weekly sessions with a psychiatrist. He was a brilliant, incisive man, immensely helpful to me at a time of alarming turmoil when I had not yet integrated the Habit of Stillness into my daily life. He helped me understand that the key to staying on top of my depression was accessing and then heeding the quiet voice of the Beloved in my core. One day he spoke of his wife, also a psychiatrist, who would not face her day without engaging in a simple ritual that took only a few minutes. She would sit in a particular rocking chair near two small casement windows facing her backyard. On any given day, she might see a bright yellow oak leaf fluttering to the ground or she might stare at a gray sky. Sometimes she would observe the birds quarreling among the denuded branches. Though someone who stayed away from organized religion, she found God-consciousness in the peace of that daily moment—a respite from the relentless activity that otherwise consumed each day.

We are all different. Despite the fact that in public I am quite gregarious, the tests that measure introversion and extroversion consistently show that I am an introvert—this means that after a certain amount of stimulation my energy level plummets. To regain my balance, I need significant quantities of solitude. My friend Susan, in contrast, is a strong extrovert. Though she is a deeply holy person, when she goes on a retreat it is virtually impossible for her to stop texting or emailing. She finds her Stillness in writing her blog in the midst of a bustling coffee shop. Surrounded by stimulation, she feels peaceful and unburdened.

There's an elderly man I have come to know who works on the landscaping around an apartment complex where some friends of mine live. James is in his early eighties with thinning hair and strong, veiny hands. Though he is usually quiet and industrious, on a few occasions I have sat with him in the shade of a gnarled and heavily pruned live oak. James spent almost 50 years as a movie and television producer. But his most treasured memories do not come from the sets he has been on or the famous actors he has worked with, rather they date back to when he was a teenager in the late 1930s, when he worked on the lawns of a private tennis club. In the early hours of the morning, he would spend hours rolling a massive concrete cylinder back and forth over the grass to compact the earth, and further hours watering with a hose, bare feet testing the moisture level of the grass.

"Everybody always asked me, didn't I think it was boring as all get out?" he said. "But I loved it. It gave me time to think, and that's what I really cared about most in life."

James explained that when he married and had children—his family was another great source of joy to him—he soon realized he couldn't afford to continue being a groundskeeper. But in all the years he worked in the creative arts, he always turned back to solitary time in the outdoors to find his equilibrium. He spent countless hours each week helping the superintendent of the apartments where he lived, working on the splendid grounds filled with a variety of native Californian trees and shrubs, and the riotous flower garden that borders the street. While his schedule did not permit a daily commitment, he always made some time to help mow, prune, or water during the week and on the weekends. As his five children grew up, he taught them these skills too, all the while working together in silence.

Another acquaintance—who rents a small Victorian house with a claw-foot tub—sets her alarm an hour early every morning before she goes off to work in the family trucking business. Her husband, friends, and co-workers are all astonished that she does not crave that extra hour for sleep but prefers a long and leisurely morning ritual.

"I draw water in the bathtub and then brew myself a cup of tea," Annette said. "It takes a while to fill the tub, and I'll pick up the paper, decide what to wear. Michael [her husband] sleeps through it all. Finally, I get in the tub and just soak for a while—twenty minutes, sometimes longer. I'll read, or I'll just lie there."

A day when she has not had time to come to Stillness is often a day fraught by a sense of having to rush and cram activities in. "I might be doing the same number of things, but I just feel different about it," she explained.

Becoming a Learner

In the end, coming to Stillness is about opening our own minds to change; it is not about changing the intentions of the Beloved. Prayer, or Stillness, is about removing any attitudes, behaviors, and dis-ease that impede our becoming aware of the Beloved's intentions. It is not about our *creating* justice, peace, health, wholeness, and inclusion, but about dismantling within us the entrapments of fear so that justice, peace, wholeness, and inclusion for all members of the human family can become real *through us as instruments*. Stillness empowers courageous vision and action.

My friend and co-worker, Theodora, introduced me to a transformative rubric for life that was developed by Betty Sue Flowers, an author and educator. In a conference Theodora attended, the presenter asked everyone to write a brief outline of their autobiography in three different ways: first as a victim, then as a hero, and finally as a learner. Those are three very different stories with three very different energies, and three very different outcomes. A victim feels the need to be defended, vindicated, or avenged. A hero needs justification, ego promotion, or validation.

And a learner? A learner seeks illumination, correction, and direction.

Learners open themselves to discovering the new in every situation, particularly challenging ones. To use a powerful phrase of Archbishop Tutu's, the victim and hero mind-sets want only to perpetuate the "safe sameness"—the predictable and familiar. This is a closed mind-set. When I'm coming to Stillness, I frequently start out feeling more like a victim or a hero. Once I relax more deeply, I know that something transformative and fear reversing is going on as I feel myself relaxing, lowering my defenses, opening up, and becoming a learner.

A member of All Saints once wrote to ask me, "If you pray for guidance from God for a difficult situation and a wonderful solution comes to you that you would never have thought of otherwise, is that grace or is that an answer to prayer?" She wanted to know what to call the phenomenon because it happens repeatedly after she receives communion.

My answer was that it is both: grace *and* authentic prayer. They are one and the same. In Stillness, in prayer, we receive grace.

The parishioner explained that when she returns to her pew after receiving communion, an image comes to mind in which the top of her head has a small door in it that opens on a hinge. Wise and important ideas and solutions come to her through this door. "I suppose this is the openness that you describe," she wrote, "and I surely have experienced God's nudges and solutions during this time."

Sometimes solutions come to us after much Stillness, and sometimes they come unbidden. But both experiences come more easily because of the open-hearted posture of the learner. One simply cannot learn when one has given oneself over to fear. A reactive, reflex-based orientation to life doesn't leave room for learning; it leaves us believing we already know everything. We can't learn what the Beloved is unfurling in our lives and in the world if we are convinced that everything significant has already been revealed to us. My father often told me when I was a teenager, "Son, it is important for you to realize that you don't know everything."

That is the entire notion of the Habit of Stillness. It is "learning prayer." It is that experience of sanity, wisdom, courage, clarity, poetry, or new perspective that comes into our open heart and mind and enlightens and transforms us.

Unlocking the Door

You may have already tried and failed to banish your *monkey thoughts*, as some Buddhists call our overactive brains. There are many days when I am sitting in my chair trying to come to Stillness and feel virtually assaulted by worries. It is my belief that trying to banish busy thoughts is counterproductive. I use a journal in which I note down concerns or ideas that occur to me as I sit in prayer. I have heard of writers who keep "morning pages" (a phrase coined by author Julia Cameron), in which they write down a stream of consciousness first thing each day to relieve their creative minds of the burden of distracting thoughts and subconscious anxieties.

A certain text, thought, or image may be the key to unlocking your own door to Stillness. Seasoned meditators in a variety of

traditions often repeat mantras over and over again in order to concentrate the mind. Practitioners of many of the world religions use
prayer beads, methodically reciting a different prayer for each bead,
to help calm their thoughts and bring them a sense of serenity. My
Muslim friend Nasirah reads the Koran aloud, randomly opening to
various passages to see what message the day might bring her. My
colleague, Catherine, reads poetry to find Stillness.

When he was in his early twenties, another friend—an atheist
deeply interested in philosophy—stumbled on an explanation of
Taoism in a book by Benjamin Hoff called *The Tao of Pooh*. Though
it seems at first glance to be a children's book, Eric has consistently
found wisdom in its pages. Now a businessman and world traveler
in his forties, Eric tucks the worn, pale-blue hardcover of this book
in his travel bag whenever he is on the road. At home he reads it
almost daily. Even after more than 20 years of reading through the
very same passages again and again, the act of regularly coming to
Stillness wherever he may be or whatever challenges he may face
gives him the peace of mind to carry on with fortitude and an open
heart.

The pressures of the everyday—"the tyranny of the urgent"—are
fundamentally egocentric, as they are really about the many responsibilities that we must bear and fulfill. When we reach Stillness, we
are moving beyond ego into a realm where those daily pressures can
be held more lightly. In doing this, we open our hearts to the miraculous power of gratitude. Anxiety we feel about having too much on
our plates can be replaced by a quiet confidence that we will meet
whatever comes with a resourceful repertoire as we are now connected to a spring of love at our core. Abraham Joshua Heschel, a
Jewish theologian and rabbi best known for his involvement in the
civil rights and antiwar movements of the 1960s and early 1970s,
wrote of the human desire to "escape from the mean and penuri-
ous, from calculating and scheming." His words can be interpreted
to reflect the yearnings and capabilities within each of us, regardless
of how we feel about God or the Beloved: "How good it is to wrap

oneself in prayer," he wrote, "spinning a deep softness of gratitude to God in all thoughts, enveloping oneself in the silk of a song."

In Stillness, we cease to be the center of the universe; instead, the Beloved within us connects to the Beloved within all humankind and we become aware that we all are truly one. In this state, we feel immense gratitude and we are energized.

As Zen Master Hakuin said, "Meditation in the midst of action is a billion times better than meditation in silence." Carrying Stillness forward is the practical way by which we can be instruments of love's peace, receiving healing for our own wounds and bringing others into the fold of love, with all its healing and empowering properties.

How to Practice Stillness

I love movies that have a "transformational rain scene." In those movies, the protagonist has a strong opinion about how his or her journey and relationships should look—but then something outside of human control takes place. A relationship ends; someone dies; tragedy strikes. The old plan now lies in the rubble. In these "trans-formational rain scenes," the character either goes for a walk in the rain or watches the rain falling outside while sipping wine, hot tea, or coffee. A decision is being made relative to what needs to be left behind and what needs to be embraced in the character's life plan. A significant midcourse correction takes place. Those who open themselves to a trajectory that is more supple, expansive, and inclusive are those whose lives bring love, joy, and wisdom to others and to the world.

We can choose to lean into the unknown with a fearless, defense-less spirit of learning, or we can resist ever coming to Stillness, or ever reflecting in the rain. Our resistance leaves us stuck within predictable and conventional fear-laced boundaries that are often marred by self-doubt, internal unrest, and an unattractive, unhelpful willfulness. Ultimately, Stillness is about listening to what the Beloved is leading us to do. We cannot even hear those things, much less have the courage to work on accomplishing them, unless we embrace the power of Stillness.

❋ Find your own mode of coming to Stillness through trial and error. There is no right or wrong way. One friend who lives near the ocean goes to stare at it, longingly and deeply, until it performs its task of being what he calls "the great eraser." My cousin Herschel is a gregarious businessman who tells hilarious stories that can make you hold your sides in pain because you are laughing so hard. He doesn't seem like someone who can feel so stressed he wants to strangle the next person he meets. When he gets this way, he goes to a sandbar in the middle of the river near where he lives and sits there until he regains his sanity and a renewed perspective. You might find Stillness in repetitive movements or in sounds, whereas others need to be stationary and silent. Some people close their eyes, some stare into space. Some come to Stillness by gazing at icons or flowers or paintings, or by watching the flickering light of a candle or a fire. Many come to Stillness through painting, making music, gardening. As we have seen, many come to Stillness reading poetry or studying some other text of wisdom or devotion. What is most important is that you persevere until you have given the silt enough time to settle to the bottom of the basin.

❋ Try sitting quietly and comfortably so your mind is free to wander. Allow your memory to visit different times and parts of your life. You are looking for occasions when you felt most deeply at peace inside, enjoying a place of loving connectedness with all that is. For myself, I remember that moment of playing alone in a pine grove as a little boy. I find this prelude to Stillness reconfigured in the experiences I have had as an adult. Ask yourself if there is anything to learn from the memory that comes to you about what your unique practice of Stillness might look like. The Habit of Stillness is most rewarding when it is integrated into your life in a proactive rather than reactive manner. Of course, like Herschel, it is helpful to know what works to unwind you when life has wound you up. The goal is to make coming to Stillness a daily habit that you grow to expect and enjoy.

✻ Give yourself at least ten minutes each day with the practice you are developing. Try to expand the amount of time you spend with your own Habit of Stillness, exercising it until the practice really becomes a habit—until it becomes an end in itself first, and *then* the secure base from which the rest of your day can become an adventure.

✻ Experiment with the times of day that work best for you. My friend Kate became extremely frustrated because she tried unsuccessfully to get into the habit of taking 20 minutes for herself first thing in the morning. During that time she was often tired and distracted, and unable to come to peace. Later she realized that early evening, when she was home from the bank and her son was at soccer practice, was a much more suitable time for her. A former colleague of mine, Dan, finds daily practice impossible, but does attend a regular yoga class two days a week. Once he has worked through all his edgy, compulsive thoughts by contorting his body for over an hour, he reaches the final pose known as Savasana (or, rather humorously, the Corpse Pose). At this point, he is so deeply relaxed and at peace that he often falls asleep. He carries this peace with him into his everyday life.

✻ How will you know when you have reached Stillness? To paraphrase Jesus, you will know it by its fruits. If you feel things are being put into perspective and you can now laugh at the hundred little mistakes of the last 24 hours, then you have come to Stillness. If you can forgive yourself and have compassion for others, then you have come to Stillness. It is my deepest hope that by going to your unique home base you will become aware of the power of love that actively, unconditionally, and undyingly dwells in each one of us.

CHAPTER THREE

The Habit of Truth

Tell all the Truth but tell it slant—
Success in Circuit lies
Too bright for our infirm Delight
The Truth's superb surprise
As Lightning to the Children eased
With explanation kind
The Truth must dazzle gradually
Or every man be blind—

—Emily Dickinson

One night after dinner I headed back to church to make a presentation to a group of people who were interested in perhaps becoming members of All Saints. At the conclusion of eight classes, if these inquirers still wish to join, our rite is for them to be baptized. If they have already been baptized they may register their baptism with All Saints.

When I walked into the room, a cluster of faces turned toward me, curious and engaged. Before I could begin talking, the parishioner leading the class posed a question that only I, as the rector of All Saints, could answer.

"There is a man in the class who is Jewish," she explained. He had been worshipping at All Saints for more than a year now and had decided that he wanted to become a member of our church, but there was a catch. "He doesn't want to be baptized."

This particular request goes against an ancient paradigm in Christianity. I knew that permitting a nonbaptized individual to officially join our congregation would cause anxiety and fear in some people, both inside and outside our church. At the same time, All Saints lives on the frontier of openness and welcome; this defines our core mission. We believe in radical inclusion. Since 9/11, we have believed that to be religious in the twenty-first century is to be interreligious. This means embracing all others with open arms, both inviting and celebrating differences, and living with the knowledge that no one religion owns "the Truth."

As these conflicting thoughts circled through my head, I paused and privately invited a moment of Stillness to come into the room and into my heart. Sometimes I have found that if the situation is immediate enough and the intent to reach Truth honest enough, it can arrive in an instant. The response that welled up almost immediately within me was *Yes, we will do it. He can join.* It was clear to me that the religion this Jewish man was experiencing in his practice with us was inclusive and compelling (after all, the word *religion* means "to re-connect") and that this should trump an exclusionary Christian convention. Since the Beloved is radically inclusive, why shouldn't we be?

I took a deep breath. This move was risky. I did not have all the ramifications worked out in advance, and oftentimes neither will you when you face your Truth. But we move forward nonetheless without those benefits; that's the nature of risk. We may encounter resistance sometime in the future, but if we sincerely believe that what we are doing is following Truth, we can be assured that we will be able to navigate any subsequent problems that may arise; that is the very nature of faith.

The essence of practicing the Habit of Truth is that we have to follow Truth, it does not follow us. Truth does not obey our plans, it *transforms* our plans, knocking down partitions and making more

room to dance in Truth's space. When we open our lives to collab-
orate with the resonance of the Beloved that flows through us, we
grasp the power of Truth.

Finding Our Internal Moral Compass

I am a theater fanatic. I love watching plays and discussing with actors the ins and outs of how they inhabit a role. Seeing an actor's
script is fascinating to me. Issued by the theater company, it has the
individual's name printed on the top: every scene that person is in is
in bold font, and each line that actor speaks is highlighted. If only
life gave us such a script! Yet while we may not receive a document
that helps us with our choices and quandaries, I do believe that the
Habit of Truth can help train us to realize which words, behaviors,
and actions "have our names on them." We can ascertain which
choices are truly ours—and which come from someone else's script
for us that we may be following out of fear.

One of the concrete strategies to start practicing the Habit of
Truth involves examining the script we have been using to guide
us. This script is made up of a set of assumptions about ourselves,
our country, our class, and our tribe. Yet Truth is not static; it represents constantly developing ideas and insights about ourselves and
the world. It is critical that we ask ourselves whether we have an
open heart or a fearful one when we are making these assumptions
about our scripts. As I myself experienced when I was in my twenties, the Habit of Truth will lead us to distinguish between them.

Growing up, I was expected to become a minister in the Southern Baptist tradition. But my father was the only kind of minister I
could envision being, and his working model of ministry included
that fear-inducing threat of eternal punishment that I simply could
not accept. As a child, I lived with the haunting fear of what
would happen if I were judged inadequate. Was this the Truth that
should be guiding my life choices?

My father's final act of Generosity toward me, combined with a powerful new narrative I discovered in college, nudged me closer to the realization that my Truth could not be exclusionary. Neither, it should be pointed out, was Jesus's practice of this habit. Whether someone chose to follow him or not, whether greeted by affirmation or the lack thereof, Jesus knew that the way of the Beloved could never be compulsive or carry the threat of punishment. This spiritual maturity on his part distinguishes his true voice from that of some texts about him, of many of his less spiritually evolved commentators, and some so-called Christian institutions that rely on the threat of punishment.

When I looked ahead at my future, it was not clear where my Truth—my own personal script—lay. As I approached graduation from college, I had no idea what to do with my life. I asked all my friends and professors what they thought I should do. A few well-intentioned people said things like, "You look like a lawyer. You talk like a lawyer. You dress and walk like a lawyer—you ought to go to law school!"

So off I went to Vanderbilt University Law School. At first I loved the study and the rigor. In my small library carrel, the beautiful order of legal theories and precedents gave me a way to lose myself in something larger than me. It didn't matter that the content was contracts, torts, criminal law, and other legal subjects. I loved studying ten hours each day and giving my mind a real workout.

Then the United States bombed Cambodia during the Vietnam War.

Antiwar demonstrations took place throughout the world, and Vanderbilt University was no exception. One afternoon I attended a rally on campus. Standing among an unsettled and growing crowd of young men and women, one of the Vanderbilt chaplains presented us with a moral challenge: the Vietnam War was being fought largely by Americans of color against people of color in Vietnam, he said. As privileged college students, protected from having to fight the war, was this a reality we were willing to tolerate?

This resonated deeply with me. Dr. Martin Luther King Jr. had made a similar statement prior to his death. Dr. King had been organizing the "Poor People's March" on Washington to challenge the nation's conscience about the slow violence inflicted by economic injustice on the lives of those who are poor. He was making unpopular and uncomfortable connections between the underserved and America's war machine. When he was assassinated on April 4, 1968, I had been profoundly moved, and so I organized several faculty members and students to participate in the march as it came through my college town.

At the rally at my graduate school, the chaplain argued that the least we could do in solidarity with those in harm's way was to figure out what we would do if we were called to fight this war—were we not protected from the draft by the privilege of being students.

When Truth awakens one's conscience, it also demands action. The moral compass inside me was trying to find its own true north. My feet took me to the chaplain's office. In answer to my question about how to figure out what I felt about war, he tossed a stapled multipage syllabus across the desk. "You might look at this list," he said.

My eyes fell on a book title as if it were choosing me. It was a simple title, *Faith and Violence* by Thomas Merton. I didn't know the author, but I did know I was supposed to read that book. Immediately, I headed to the campus bookstore, found the book on the shelves, took it back to my carrel in the library, and began reading.

Each paragraph acted like a falling domino until my mind willingly suspended any resistance and I was relaxed in my desk chair, devouring the book. Truth sometimes comes through reading another person's work; many of us have had the experience Bob Dylan describes as hearing words pouring off the page as though they had been written in his soul. Merton's thinking, in short time, became a north star for my own journey with the Habit of Truth. Like Jesus, he trusted Truth's lead without fear. Because Merton was a man of my century, I learned from his thinking that I could do the same.

Searching for my own Truth, for the script that really had *my* name on it, I had stumbled upon this text that would help steer me in the right direction for the rest of my life.

The Journey Toward Truth

That book was the first of a half dozen volumes of Merton I consumed in the next seven months. I placed them next to my legal texts on the shelf of the library carrel and read them daily. After a few months, I was reading more Merton than law. It was the beginning of my long journey away from the script my parents and culture had written for me—and also, after college, the script that I had mistakenly thought had my name on it. Merton communicated that salvation had nothing to do with escaping hell. Rather, he explained that it was important to know that at our creation, the Beloved had placed inside each of us our true word. This word is a part of the Beloved and cannot be fabricated by us to suit our preferences. Salvation is discovering that true word.

I was beginning to understand that rather than being something we possess, Truth leads us. A life that is vibrant, vital, loving, and not based on fear is one that follows Truth. Truth is that part of the Beloved that constantly helps us grow—and in so doing, calls us to abandon the restrictive and anxiety-producing old truths by which we may have lived before. As William Sloane Coffin, a Christian clergyman and peace activist, eloquently said, "Truth is error burnt up."

Though our most celebrated sages and prophets may indeed have received Truth, it cannot be totally contained in the creeds, books, religions, or philosophies created in their name—much to the chagrin of fundamentalists in any tradition who want to believe that they own an exclusive Truth. It couldn't be, because the kind of Truth I'm talking about is more verb than noun. "Seekers of truth can build communities of love," wrote Coffin. "Possessors of truth have too much enmity toward those who don't possess the truth, or possess some other truth."

In my daily life as a preacher, there always is a moment between when I have conceived a sermon and when I deliver it during which I have to give up *my* idea of the sermon in the service of the Beloved's idea of that sermon. That is a painful and also exhilarating moment of submission to Truth. But once I've gone through that transition, my fear evaporates and I am able to stand in the pulpit with energy and courage.

Leonard Cohen, the great musician and songwriter, says in the documentary *I'm Your Man* that it is not until he gives up his idea of composing a masterpiece that *the masterpiece* of a song can be born. "Abandon your masterpiece," he says. "Sink into the real master-piece."

This then begs the question: If the first part of the Habit of Truth is that we are following Truth on a lifelong journey, where is it that we are headed?

We follow Truth to freedom, an insight contained in the biblical phrase "the truth will set you free" (John 8:32 NIV). There have been some entertaining variations on this phrase, including one attributed to the southern author Flannery O'Connor: "The truth will set you free, but first it will make you odd." Oftentimes, the journey toward Truth forces us to restructure our thinking and our lives in key ways.

Mark Twain explored this in his classic tale, *The Adventures of Huckleberry Finn*. This story etches in bold relief one of the original sins of the United States: racism heinously fueled by the institution of slavery. During the journey of Huck Finn's moral awakening, he makes a Truth-oriented breakthrough despite the culture of fear surrounding him and his friend Jim, who is a slave. Religion had conspired with the institution of slavery to promote the delusion that black people are chattel to be owned rather than human be-ings to be loved and befriended. The instrument religion employs is the well-known, oft-used, and fear-based threat we talked about earlier that seeks to keep individuals in line with the prevailing cultural norms—the threat of hell.

Huck's friend Jim escapes. Huck knows where the slave is; though his love-based self tells him to keep this knowledge secret, this would make him an accomplice to the crime. Huck actually feels his racism-distorted conscience "grinding" him, telling him that he is "wicked" for considering supporting a man's escape to freedom.

To relieve the unbearable anxiety storming Huck's soul, he decides to write a letter turning Jim in. He is willing to instigate someone else's destruction in order to calm the storm inside. That is at the essence of fear-based thinking: the sacrifice of someone else's life for mine. Love, in stark contrast, helps us see that all lives are equally precious.

In a moment of Stillness, during which Huck conjures up Jim's image and is reminded of his essential humanity, his crisis of conscience reverses. He picks up the letter: "I was a-trembling, because I'd got to decide, forever, betwixt two things, and I knowed it. I studied a minute, sort of holding my breath, and then says to myself: 'All right, then, I'll go to hell'—and tore it up." He decides, "I would go to work and steal Jim out of slavery again; and if I could think up anything worse, I would do that, too; because as long as I was in, and in for good, I might as well go the whole hog."

That moment is a universal one in which the Habit of Truth leads us from fear to love. It shows us how extreme fear—in this case, going against cultural norms and therefore being sent to hell—can distort the human conscience and even reality. But in purifying our conscience, the Habit of Truth uses us as a conduit to correct the prejudices and injustices of a fear-based culture. When we hear its call, it prods us to action.

The Courage to Act

Each one of us experiences our own moments of Truth. Huck's moment came when in Stillness he contemplated his friend and realized that he needed to lean against the prevailing wind in order to make his own way toward Truth. These moments can be highly dramatic or they can happen in a quiet, albeit defining, way.

Parents often talk about recognizing the "Truth" of their children, which can be quite different from the image they nurtured. Sometimes children struggle mightily as they mature to be recognized as having their own Truth. When I was traveling with my son, Peter, looking at colleges, I realized I was striding through those campuses narrating the journey enthusiastically according to my Truth. He and I are not the same; his Truth is different from mine. When I realized this, I slowed down and let him take the lead in uncovering what was most meaningful to him.

But however Truth comes, it bears with it just enough of its own sense of rightness to overcome the fear of risk taking. While genuine risk plays a crucial role in all of the Habits of Love, it is perhaps most keen in the Habit of Truth. At too many forks in the road, anxiety stops us from following Truth's suggested direction. What will happen if I say *yes* to Truth as I recognize it? That question can arrest us in our tracks. Then, at other moments of choice, Truth breaks through.

In law school, I became aware that I was living a lie. It began earlier when I read Thomas Merton's work, but even then I was not sure where Truth was trying to lead me. Later, on a clear and sunny day, I was driving by the law school listening to a radio program about graduates from law schools and other graduate programs. Suddenly a thought came to me out of the blue: *You will never graduate from Vanderbilt Law School.* It was like feeling the first drops of rain falling and trying to convince yourself that there's not a storm coming.

Sometimes I believe this is the Beloved's way of preparing us to see life in a new way, by suggesting in a murmur the outline of a future collaboration. But the Beloved is also gracious; love doesn't give us only one chance to perceive Truth and then we've missed it forever. Every day presents an opportunity to get on course. "In every event there is something sacred at stake," wrote the Jewish scholar Abraham Joshua Heschel. We don't only get one moment to decide.

If that voice I heard while listening to the radio was the beginning of inclement weather, the storm definitely picked up strength heading into the final exams for that fall semester. I had learned the Uniform Commercial Code out of love for the professor who delighted in teaching, more so than for the love of the Code itself. A stickler for precision, this professor insisted that we use the first two hours of the four-hour exam outlining our answers to the test questions. In fact, he interpreted our signing the honor pledge on the cover of the small blue examination books as an oath that we had not begun writing until the beginning of the third hour.

I crafted an intricate outline for my answers. It took about an hour and forty-five minutes, after which my legs needed a stretch. I took a break and went for a brief walk in the lightly falling snow of a beautiful January morning. Then it happened.

A quiet voice asked me, *Are you an attorney?*

I walked silently and after a while another voice within me answered, "No."

If you are not an attorney, do you need a law degree?

Silence. Then from my depths came the answer, "No."

If you do not need a law degree, do you need to finish this exam?

The "No" that followed that question came more quickly than its predecessors.

I kept walking and never went back into that examination room. A huge set of complications followed that epiphany in the snow—with my fiancée (now wife), my parents, the law school, the law professor who later found me (and after my explanation understood on a level that to this day surprises me). But none of the complications were daunting. Painful and uncomfortable for others and for me, yes; overwhelming, no. Complications have a tendency to fall into place when we become clear about our course, when we have no doubt that Truth has led us in charting that course.

This brings me back to the story with which I opened the chapter: my decision to allow the Jewish man to join our congregation without being baptized. Years later, I now know that all my anxiety about whether or not to include this worshipper was wasted energy, which of course is what most worry does — it wastes energy. No second shoe dropped. In fact, quite the opposite has taken place. This man has found his role as a warm and smiling usher for worship services. His presence in our midst has been thoroughly positive. Whenever any member learns that he is Jewish, they smile their approval. One person said, "It's great to have a member from the same religion Jesus practiced."

One Person's Truth vs. Another's

One of the trickiest aspects of the Habit of Truth is that Truth is a matter of perspective rather than fact. Whenever we ask ourselves, "What is the Truth of this situation..." we should always add on to the end of that question, "...*for me?*" This is not to say that Truth is individualistic and leads us without concern for the impact on the greatest good for everyone. However, we must start with exercising personal responsibility for thinking through Truth's call to us without insisting that others answer this question in the exact same way we do.

This can lead to great emotional upheaval in our lives. When we perceive a Truth that others do not, we must find a way to bridge that gap — or we must accept those differences and learn how we can best live with them. This may mean turning away from someone we have cherished, or it may mean embracing someone whose Truth differs from our own.

Relationships with our family members are among the deepest, most complex, and longest-lasting relationships we have. Yet families are also where the Habit of Truth can be played out in the most painful and confusing ways. I know of a young woman named Julia who has been struggling since she was a teenager with anxiety and depression. A few years ago, she suffered a series of such debilitating panic attacks that she was forced to look closely at her past and her own behavior to determine what was causing her such enduring pain and fear. Through the arduous process of psychotherapy combined with a return to healing activities such as yoga, daily walks with her husband, and painting, she began to understand what had been happening.

The youngest child in her family, Julia had always had a very close relationship with her father, a well-known teacher in their hometown in Ohio. Once her older siblings were out of the house, she and her father became even closer and spent most weekends together working on projects around the house. Julia moved back to Ohio after college, living just a few blocks from her parents. She started her own family, and everything seemed fine. Then her only child, a daughter, became a teenager. That's when the panic attacks started.

It took a while, but Julia eventually realized that to become healthy again, she had to acknowledge that her relationship with her father was dysfunctional. A magnetic personality, he wielded a disproportionate amount of power over her. Even as an adult, she sought to please him at every turn. As she watched him interact with her 14-year-old, she could not shake a pervading sense of unease. Something about the intensity of his attention made her deeply uncomfortable. Though there was no violence or coercion between them, he was an overwhelming force. Once she recognized this Truth—one she knew few others would understand or even recognize—she felt an immense burden lift from her. For years she had been telling herself that these feelings were wrong, and now she was acknowledging her Truth and accepting it as valid and meaningful.

For Julia, this Truth was one that was difficult to face because it upset her understanding of how the world works. Acting on this Truth was risky, as it had the potential to disrupt her life even further—would she confront her father? Move away? Create physical or emotional distance between them? Also, she was aware that this was a Truth others might not share, and this made her feel isolated and fearful.

In families and in other relationships—but also in religion, politics, and foreign policy—we cause ourselves and others so much pain, anxiety, and fear by trying to defend old, toxic worldviews that are nothing but error, or our individualistic constrictive versions of "the truth." Once we follow Truth into something more life giving and sustaining for everyone, we are more at ease; we can at that moment become more our loving, open selves. Our true selves.

Gandhi said, "An error does not become truth by reason of multiplied propagation, nor does truth become error because nobody sees it." Julia was caught in a web of fear and guilt, and only when she was able to rewrite her script and accept her own narrative of what lay beneath her family's relationships was she able to be free of the burden of her crushing anxiety. In this case, the process of recognizing her Truth meant she was already acting upon it in her soul.

The Journey Is Ongoing

Practicing the Habit of Truth is not a one-time exercise. The issue is how we keep fear from fogging everything up, obscuring the way forward once we've changed paths. When parents accept, for example, that their child must follow another route than the one they had imagined and charted out, letting go of that past Truth seems terrifying; the stakes are so very high. But recognizing that the path has

changed because it is guided by Truth helps anxious parents let go
of their script.

In making decisions regarding our own actions, fear can still
invade us after Truth has pointed the way toward an authentic, dif-
ferentiated life grounded in love. That fear confuses us, infecting
us with the most perplexing doubts. Every time fear tempts us to
abandon course, the Beloved again invites us to practice the Habit
of Truth. The pattern of charting our authentic course—marked by
wavering confidence and external resistance, and culminating in a
deepened commitment to that which has our name on it—has been
a familiar experience to all spiritual seekers, including Jesus at the
time of his temptation in the desert.

I myself learned this lesson at a point of great vulnerability.
(Aren't most of our great experiential lessons learned at points of
personal vulnerability?) I had abandoned law and trained to become an Episcopal minister. Now it was urgent that I find a paying
job. What to do? Where to go? My bishop sent me to check out a
few options. The first was clearly a mismatch—but the second priest
I met with seemed a match made in heaven.

Dan Matthews was a driven, imaginative, highly successful,
media-savvy and media-loving circus ringmaster of a priest. Prayerful and holy to be sure, but far too earthly and busy to be confined
in stained glass. I loved him—and I loved the idea of being trained
by him.

Dan offered me a job in his church, St. Luke's, in Atlanta—
a bright star in the firmament of progressive and socially relevant
urban churches. I feared, however, that the southern conservative
prejudice against those critical of American foreign policy might
eclipse the liberal positions St. Luke's board members had taken on
civil rights, feeding the hungry, and caring for the homeless. Only
15 years earlier, the Atlanta powerful had judged Martin Luther
King Jr. as taking things too far when, in his critique of the Vietnam
War, he made a connection between American racism and American foreign policy. I had found Dr. King's connection to be true

and, four years later, declared myself a conscientious objector to war in any form. The question I had for Dan Matthews was whether in my interview with the board of his church I should reveal that I was a conscientious objector.

In his wisdom, Dan said that it was up to me. He felt that it could go either way. They might overlook it or it might ruin my chances. It was my call. In other words, the risk was mine.

Moments of fork-in-the-road fear have a way of searing themselves in one's memory. I became very still inside in order to have that all-important conversation with myself and with the Beloved. I asked myself, *Is this part of my story so crucial to who I am and what I believe about life and about the course I have charted that I need to express it—bear witness to it—no matter what?*

The church's board included some of the most handsomely attired women and men I had ever seen, Atlanta's finest both in character and in sartorial excellence. During our lengthy meeting, I tried to mirror the same. The exchange went swimmingly. I started considering all of the positive benefits that would flow from being hired: my family would enjoy my dependable revenue to add to my wife Hope's full-time salary; the mortgage payments could be made; I could have a great church and a resourceful priest as my first training ground in the Episcopal Church. And yet—it could all evaporate in one confession: "I object to war in any form." At the same time, I had a sense that this moment could determine whether or not I would forever hide my ethical convictions in the service of getting or keeping a job.

Was I going to operate from my fearful self or my open-hearted self?

"There is one more thing…" I began.

Did Dan Matthews just look at me askance? Did his facial expression say, "Why screw it up now, boy? You've got it in the bag!" Or was I projecting onto him my father's disapproval? Or was that perhaps my own fear making itself known? The parliament of selves inside me were yelling all at the same time.

Thank the Beloved, I decided to tell the story of coming to terms with what I thought was the destructive impracticality of war to solve international problems. The room became tranquil, as did my interior parliament of selves. I was surprisingly peaceful and relaxed, no longer attached to the results after hearing Truth whisper in my ear.

The gentle, patrician board chair said something both professional and liberating like, "It will be good to have a young man on our staff who has thought so carefully about an important moral issue of our time."

How to Practice Truth

It is important to remember that Truth is not a set of ideas anyone can memorize or systematize and then expect to earn some sort of certificate of accomplishment. Truth cannot be fully contained in one's mind, words, concepts, or thoughts—it is too alive, vast, and out of human control for that. Rather, Truth is a constantly unfolding series of insights, understandings, revelations, and epiphanies about ourselves and how the world works.

Not only do we learn from Truth until we take our last breath, but it has the potential to galvanize change on a large scale. Boston University professor Andrew Bacevich, a highly respected thinker on foreign policy, discovered late in life that the truths he had accumulated over a 20-year career as a soldier—especially about the Cold War—were not entirely true at all. During a walk in Berlin after the fall of the wall, he encountered off-duty Russian soldiers peddling badges, medallions, hats, bits of uniforms, and other artifacts of the supposedly fierce and mighty Red Army. It was all cheap junk. "I started, however hesitantly, to suspect that orthodoxy might be a sham. I began to appreciate that authentic truth is never simple and that any version of truth handed down from on high—whether by presidents, prime ministers, or archbishops—is inherently suspect," he wrote.

Truth always leads us to a greater capacity for both self *and* others. Bacevich was moved to share with others his radically altered thinking on the nature of Truth, and in so doing has influenced a generation of thinkers toward an understanding of the world based less in fear and more in love. Naturally, Truth leads us to a more vital and honest life for ourselves, but only in the service of releasing more vitality for all of creation. Truth seeks to rearrange the life of the individual so there is more compassion, justice, sustainability, and peace for all.

The reason we cannot permanently possess Truth is because it does not exist prior to being manifest. That is both the frightening and the thrilling aspect of Truth. Letting Truth lead you to embrace your loved and loving self can therefore be a scary proposition—on the surface of things. You may experience a combination of exhilaration, fright, and loneliness that seems too much to bear and tempts you to go back to a predictable, safe, and comfortable life in which you operated from your fearful self. Yet when we follow Truth into an open-hearted life, our experiences are incredibly magnetic and profoundly fortifying. Truth will always break any mold that binds it.

* The Habit of Truth cannot lead us well unless we have an inner and deep sense of calm. Do you remember my parishioner from the Habit of Stillness who reported the sensation of a door opening in the top of her head and important "ideas and solutions" coming in? This is known as the "still, small voice" that speaks directly to the individual in the prophetic tradition. Jesus repeatedly "went aside," from being with others, even his chosen small group of twelve. This deeply imprinted practice of Stillness—one of Jesus's habits—was so noticeable that all the chroniclers of his life mention it. When seeking to practice Truth, therefore, first give time for the Habit of Stillness to take you into the calm center of your life.

* If you think you have come to your center and yet you still find turmoil there, then give yourself more Stillness. The likelihood is that

you have not yet come to your true center. That is okay—it may not yet be the right time. Sometimes it takes hours and sometimes, in some situations, it may take days, weeks, or months to come to that place of Stillness—particularly when the Habit of Truth is involved.

🌸 When you have accessed your point of Stillness, try to phrase the topic you want to consider in the light of Truth into a short, open-ended sentence. What is the issue that you are asking your loving self to inform? You may hear conflicting internal opinions about your chosen subject; when you do, ask yourself these questions:

1. Does the Truth that you are hearing exclude a particular religion, tribe, or group of people or does it move toward turning the human race into the human family? Remember: the deepest goal in practicing the Habits of Love is to know how deeply the Beloved treasures you and every other human being.

2. Does the Truth that you are hearing have the potential to bring you into conflict? Every time we make a stride in following Truth, there is some form of conflict—either internally with one's self or externally with one's family, friends, institutions, or culture (or both). Such a conflict often comes from the collision of two competing stories, one based in fear, the other based in love. Try to identify the two stories out of which the conflict is arising.

3. Does one of these two stories seem to be more deeply rooted in fear? Who represents the fear-based story? What is their relationship to you? If you depart from their script for your life, what do you imagine you might suffer? Though you might

justifiably fear the disapproval or disappointment of your family or friends (as I did), ask yourself whether their censure is worse than the reality of living a life that is not true to yourself.

4. Turn now to the other, love-based story. Is that story accompanied by a calm, if faint, confidence? In words or attitude you may feel something like the following: "I know that my course of action is not one that so-and-so would choose for me and it may go against so-and-so's set of values. I have now come to understand that I must choose this new way or else do violence to my own heart and conscience." Continue to evaluate the truthfulness of the love-based story by considering that the other by-products of Truth besides confidence are peace, joy, patience, kindness, self-control, and generosity of spirit.

* Know that you are not alone in needing to find the courage to go against others' expectations of you. Reach out to people who have had similar experiences. Listen to and learn from their stories.

* Recognize that no Truth can be entirely free of fear. My mentor, Rabbi Friedman, taught me that we may sometimes have to temporarily cut off relations with others in order to establish a healthier foundation for resuming that connection later. This can be a way of affirming that you are, in fact, open to the possibility of building a love-based relationship in the future, but to do so you must turn away from the old, destructive narrative for a while.

* At times, living with our Truth will seem risky and alienating. We may struggle and need to take a hard look at why we do what we do and why we believe what we believe. Throughout our lives, when Truth leads us to a new level of understanding and defines our lives and our values, it often informs us that we are about to be trans-

formed by setting up some internal conflict. If you experience this
struggle and confusion, remember that this conflict is never the last
word. The last word is a newfound and deeply founded peace and
fortification to live our lives free from fear and in the embrace of our
loving selves.

CHAPTER FOUR

The Habit of Candor

Not the high mountain monastery
I had hoped for, the real
face of my spiritual practice
is this:
the sweat that pearls on my cheek
when I tell you the truth...

—Kim Rosen

Reverend Al Sharpton and Professor Cornel West—two social activists who have long been in the spotlight fighting for civil rights— are old friends. For decades they have both, in fundamentally different ways, sought to address and alleviate the racial inequities of our society. Recently, they sat under the bright lights on national television, debating the current state of the African American agenda. While they have historically been allies, here they became, briefly, adversaries. But in the midst of their raucous disagreement, they were unwittingly practicing the Habit of Candor. It is this Candor that allowed them to continue their discussion constructively in other forums, deepening the debate and serving as a way forward rather than a dead end of disagreement.

The panel was talking about the extent to which President Obama and other black elected officials should be held accountable to an African American agenda, and the debate became heated as opinions clashed. Sharpton and West both felt strongly and argued their opposing positions passionately. Sharpton energetically supported President Obama's record. West, however, not only felt Obama had been weak in improving the lives of those who are poor while protecting the elite, but also questioned Sharpton's objectivity and freedom to offer a critique, given that he had recently taken a high-profile job in the media. Voices were raised and fingers pointed; it was uncomfortable for those unfamiliar with the benefits and skills of frank debate. The other panelists looked on in silence, and the moderator sat back momentarily and allowed the two friends to hash it out on live TV.

What was remarkable was not so much the details of the disagreement, nor the fact that these two were allowed the time to argue vociferously—when moderated news shows typically deal in bite-size segments presenting, politely, various differences of opinion. What was astonishing was the rare display of Candor. In this instance, these two men entered into the kind of courageous conversation in which words of substance and import were exchanged. Friends for many years, West often prefaced his categorical disagreements with "Brother," and he stated up front, "I loved this brother when he was on the outside, I love this brother when he is on the inside," referring to Sharpton's status inside and outside the circles of the mainstream media.

The incident reveals skillful handling of the most problematic element of the Habit of Candor: how to voice an opinion that may unbalance, anger, or put on the defensive the person you are addressing. But therein lies the beauty of this habit—successfully engaging Candor leads us to recognize and value the preciousness and durability of the relationship we have with the person with whom we are disagreeing. The fact that we can share a different perspective and still respect one another is among the highest compliments we can pay someone.

All of us experience similar moments of decision when our hearts are beating fast; something on our minds and in our hearts needs expression, yet we are afraid giving voice to this will be harmful to ourselves, to others, or to our relationships. Will we swallow what we have to say out of fear and risk its slipping out later in a distorted and maybe even destructive manner? Or will we express it forthrightly, calling on our own internal maturity and the maturity of the other person or persons? When we engage the Habit of Candor, our open, loving hearts help alleviate our fear and give us the courage to speak our minds. In fact, in using our words to engage in courageous conversations, we not only express ourselves without debilitating fear but we also achieve great benefit and even transformation.

Using Your Words

The Hebrew scriptures tell the story of a beautiful woman named Bathsheba who, late one afternoon as the sun begins to set, is bathing on the roof of her house while the curtains around her flutter in the wind. On the walls of the palace compound stands King David, watching her with awe and desire. He sends his guards to fetch the woman, who is the wife of an Israelite soldier fighting at the Siege of Rabbah. The king and Bathsheba make love and she becomes pregnant with his child. To cover up what he has done, the king arranges for her husband, Uriah, to be brought back from harm's way for a conjugal visit with his wife. But when this plan fails, King David moves Uriah to the front lines of the conflict; under the king's orders, Uriah is deserted by his men in the middle of a bloody battle and is killed.

During this time, about a thousand years before the birth of Jesus, it was common for royalty to pay court prophets to tell them what they wanted to hear. But during King David's reign, there lived a man named Nathan who came from the genuine prophetic tradition that calls for prophets not to be "yes men."

Though King David is the most powerful man in the ancient world, Nathan feels compelled to tell his king that his actions were inexcusable, and that he must take responsibility for Uriah's murder. With great fortitude he faces the king and recounts a parable about a rich man who steals a poor man's beloved pet sheep. Appalled by the story, King David agrees that the rich man has acted heinously and must be punished. At Nathan's prodding, the king sees his own moral error as reflected in Nathan's story.

"Why have you despised the word of God to do what is evil in his sight?" Nathan asks, connecting the dots explicitly. "You are the man." This biblical story has fueled five thousand years of the prophetic value of "speaking truth to power."

While Nathan's story may have been one of the first recorded examples of speaking truth to power, it is no different than what some of our most universally candid people—Tolstoy, Gandhi, Eleanor Roosevelt, Martin Luther King Jr., and the Dalai Lama—have exercised, resulting in less violence in our world. That is the trick to "using your words," and using them well, as we will see.

Children who are fighting are always being told, "Use your words, not your fists!" As most adults know, getting kids to express themselves verbally reduces aggression and alleviates tension much more effectively than when they respond physically. But when we grow up we don't always follow our own advice. Oftentimes, rather than forthrightly and carefully working through our differences, we walk on eggshells or avoid contact altogether at uncomfortable junctures. This leads either to stasis or to a growing, unexpressed anger and resentment that feeds our fearful selves and starves our loving selves.

Moving from Fear to Love

Fear-based avoidance of frank conversations sets us up to act out our resentments or other difficult feelings. Then there is too much room for misunderstanding and even retaliation. Silences invite wild misinterpretations and crazy-making assumptions. But finding the skillful way and the opportune time to use our words to get at the heart of the matter cuts through the fear that all these resentments and misunderstandings represent.

Hope and I had a particularly instructive experience of Candor in regard to a long sermon I was working on in which I focused on my relationship with Hope's mother, now deceased. She was a significant character in many defining moments early in our marriage. My relationship with her was one of the most challenging and enriching of my life, so it taught me lessons of immense value that I wanted to share with others. It was important to me to seek Hope's permission to describe her mother and our interactions as I had. One morning I gave Hope a draft of the sermon to read before I went to work. She and I planned to talk that afternoon.

On my way home, fear rose in my body and my heart started beating fast. My breathing became shallow. I had a bitter taste in my throat. A hundred fear-based, worst-case scenarios rushed through my mind: Hope would be angry at me; she would be hurt and not speak to me; she would resent my exhuming a painful time in our lives; she would be weeping over how I had described her mother; I would lose her affection. Fear that runs rampant in the echo chamber of conversations we have with ourselves can manufacture a million catastrophic fantasies.

In a matter of minutes during that drive home, I remembered that just the day before while coming to Stillness, I had experienced fear literally melting away as I called to mind the victim-hero-learner distinctions. Being a victim or a hero leads us to be closed minded, whereas when we are a learner we are open hearted— recognizing that we may need correction or illumination. My entire day had been recolored as I imagined entering fear-inducing meetings with the attitude of a learner. I realized that I could receive Hope's comments as a victim or a hero or a learner. I could be defensive, hurt, or falsely humble—or I could receive what she had to say, engage it in the spirit of gaining what I could learn from it, and improve the sermon at the same time.

I found her sitting on the patio with the pages of my draft on the table before her. "You must be carrying a lot of pain around after all these years," she said gently.

"Yes," I said, relaxing immediately. "That's true."

Pointing to one paragraph, she went on. "I think that this particular word choice is unfair." She offered some alternatives. She noted other places and again suggested a few words of her own as options. I was stunned that her proposals revealed even more than my initial attempts—they were perfect. I learned. I think she learned. The heart of our relationship was deepened and enriched. I "felt" her sensitivities and she "felt" mine. I felt the Beloved that dwells deeply in each of us.

The Habit of Candor means using our words so we give voice to our loving selves in such a way that the other party to the conversation can more easily move from his or her fearful self to a loved and loving self. This is what Hope helped me achieve that day.

Candor Requires Courage

Not all exercises of Candor speak truth to an earthly power like political, economic, or religious authorities. We may not feel like we are in a Nathan-type situation, but that same long walk he took into the temple to face the king is the same long walk we make to the office of a boss or the same plea we make to a person whom we love when things are not going well. Many potentially life-giving experiences of Candor are self-sabotaged by the fear that the person you are addressing will leave, in either a temporary yet uncomfortable manner or perhaps permanently, and you will be left alone in the world. While this fear is not groundless, it need not hold us back from making thoughtful decisions about when and how to use Candor. When we make these kinds of difficult decisions with an open heart, we find ourselves instinctively gathering the necessary courage to face those fears with a balance of determination and discernment. We learn to figure out whether those fears are really warranted. Through accessing our creativity and sensitivity, we can minimize the risk of alienating others. We trust that the skillful use of words can deepen a relationship, a family, a business, a religious community, or any other system, and make it even more durable.

Even when the intention of Candor is positive, people often react to it with ferocious defensiveness. The experience of a friend of mine named Mary reveals how critical it is for both parties to engage in exchanges with open hearts. Ultimately, these exchanges are in the service of helping a relationship grow deeper and even more secure. Mary is married to a burly and thoughtful graphic artist named Gus. For some years they ran their own small business, and for the past decade Mary has been in publishing and Gus has worked as a freelancer.

They have one of the most tender relationships I have witnessed, and they have great respect for one another. But when Mary had a falling out with one of her colleagues it became a strain on her marriage. She carried the frustration of daily tension home with her into her family life. An editor named Jill, with whom she was collaborating on a book project, resented Mary for her hard-driving work attitude, and felt she was controlling and ungrateful. In an unexpected and embarrassing public argument in the cafeteria one day, Jill called Mary a "slave driver" and accused her of ruining the atmosphere at work. Soon it became evident that Jill had been talking negatively about Mary to their colleagues and had even called some of their mutual acquaintances outside work to complain.

Mary, of course, saw things quite differently. Also exasperated, she had often complained to Gus that Jill was sloppy and lazy at work. It was a dagger to her heart to think that her co-workers might believe what Jill was saying about her. At home after this public and humiliating argument, sitting across from her husband at the kitchen table, Mary fully expected him to take her side. She was not only furious but she also felt personally and professionally betrayed. Most of all, she thought it was obvious that an unforgivable injustice had been visited upon her. "It's just not *fair!*" she complained.

Gus knew Mary's colleagues quite well from years of designing book jackets. And to her amazement, he did not take her side. "This has nothing to do with fairness," he said. He told his wife that she did amazing work, that he believed in her talent and admired her work ethic. But he also said that she was indeed a taskmaster and could come across as too driven and too detail oriented, especially in the office.

As we see here, the Habit of Candor entails engaging in courageous conversations about difficult things that we would often prefer to remain unspoken. In following Truth, we always encounter two realities that exist side by side: our own feelings that send us messages and the feelings of others that of course inform their understanding of their place in the world. In this exchange, Jill, Mary, and Gus all wrestled with their own Truths and with coming to an understanding of how to speak those Truths candidly. Every event can be seen from different perspectives—the Habit of Candor acknowledges this fact, while also honoring our Truth.

Mary wept while sitting at that table. She felt as though Gus was not supporting her, and this seemed to be yet another betrayal that she did not deserve. Eventually, however, as her husband continued to talk, it dawned on her that he had always wanted only the best for her and would continue to do so, and that in this disagreement his support was taking an unexpected and deeper form. When she took that step back and embraced the attitude of a learner rather than victim, she was able to see that Gus was conveying a Truth that was difficult to hear, no matter who it came from.

Thinking back over emails and meetings, she began to see things more from Jill's perspective, without totally negating her own opinion that Jill was not a dedicated worker. But just because Mary was driven did not mean that Jill had to be as driven as she was. This recognition and, ultimately, acceptance of her colleague's work style was an act of Generosity on Mary's part that allowed her to see the interaction with completely fresh eyes—to interpret it from the viewpoint of her loving self rather than her fearful self.

Quite unexpectedly, she began to feel more empowered. She could change her habits; she could improve her style and succeed even more at work. Gus's Candor at a moment of great vulnerability was in fact quite brave, as it risked alienating his wife even further and breaking their mutual trust. Instead, he managed to turn Jill's angry criticism into a constructive, fruitful, and ultimately loving gesture. His use of Candor illustrates the power of one of love's habits to make a relationship even more secure.

When Candor Backfires

No doubt it is a tricky endeavor to get Candor right. There may be instances when it is simply not practical to be candid—perhaps we ourselves are not in a loving space or we are dealing with a person or an entity that is not able to treat it as a learning experience. The other person cannot receive our words of Candor, no matter how kindly they are meant, without feeling attacked. This defensive posture is very common: we instinctively wish to protect ourselves from criticism and emotional injury.

A young woman I know named Rachel has three children under the age of six. Her parents live across the country in Vermont and every few months they visit, staying in the guest room of her compact split-level for a week or two. Rachel's mother, Ute, is an adoring grandmother with boundless energy. When she swoops in, she takes over much of the cooking and shopping, and runs errands that Rachel (a part-time accountant) has not been able to get to. A dynamo of activity, Ute is immensely helpful to her daughter. But for two years trouble has been brewing.

Ute has very set ideas about nutrition, entertainment, and clothing. While Rachel and her husband, Dan, are more laid back as parents and don't believe in sweating the small things, her mother is a take-control type of person who wants everything to be perfect. When she stays with her daughter and son-in-law, she offers a relentless stream of advice. Over time, this has increasingly made Rachel's parenting more difficult instead of easier, and has strained her relationship with Dan.

One early evening, Ute returned from an errand to find her son-in-law ensconced in his favorite chair watching television. At his feet were the kids, playing with Legos; Rachel was upstairs taking a shower. Ute stormed over, switched the TV off, and asked whether the children had even been bathed and fed yet. Dumbfounded, Dan retreated, but he and Rachel decided that during that visit they needed to address the issue and finally lay down some important ground rules. Things had to change.

The discussion did not go well. A few days later, after the children were put to bed—and Rachel's father had signed off for the night—she, Dan, and Ute stood in the kitchen talking. Rachel was fidgety and nervous.

"I love having you visit, Mom," she started, smiling tentatively. "You help a lot, and that's incredibly generous. But Dan and I, we're starting to feel like kids in our own home."

Ute frowned and folded her arms across her chest. "Well, really," she said after a moment, "you two do tend to act like kids in your own home, don't you?"

Rachel exchanged glances with Dan and tried again. "It's great that you help, but the children need to look to us as the authority here. I mean, we're the ones who are the parents when you leave to go home. Right?"

When Ute remained silent, Rachel continued trying to calmly explain her perspective. Her reasoning was solid and her tone nonconfrontational, but Ute could see nothing but criticism and ingratitude in her daughter's Candor.

Ute flushed bright red and finally said, "All right, if that's the way you feel!" and went upstairs.

The remaining days of the visit were strained. A few months went by without word of when the next visit would be. When Rachel brought it up on the phone, her mother demurred and explained that they had decided to go on a holiday elsewhere. They see much less of each other now, and have not been able to broach the topic again to try to heal the wounds. While Dan is relieved, Rachel feels the loss acutely. "But if I ask myself, should I have kept quiet, my answer is no," she explained. "I needed her to change her behavior, and if she can't do that, ultimately she loses out."

Often, in exchanges of Candor the success of the interaction can depend on external issues such as timing and location. These courageous conversations are more fruitful when undertaken on neutral territory, on a one-to-one basis, and after a cooling-off period. But even when we take all the precautions we can think of, behaving with open hearts and a generous spirit, the exchange can result in wounded feelings. When a colleague, friend, child, or spouse reacts badly to Candor, it leaves *us* feeling rejected. It may even threaten our position at work or make our personal lives tense.

It is not within our power to determine or direct how someone else will react to our actions. Naturally, we can influence others somewhat by making sensitive, loving choices, but we cannot be responsible for their feelings. At times, we must accept that doing the best we can will not lead to a breakthrough. In those instances, making an honest effort to engage in the Habit of Candor with an attitude of love needs to be enough, in and of itself.

"Authenticity" Is Complex

Practicing Candor cannot be achieved without some expression of love, be it the kind of love we have for our dearest relations or a more professional level of respect (respect is one of the manifestations of love). Since the goal is to be heard for what you are truly saying and to hear others in the same manner, Candor and Generosity are inextricably linked. If you are seeking to impose your "truth" or power on someone else through criticism or judgment, then you are engaging in a power play over that person. If the underlying motive of the exchange is to score points or establish righteousness (a hero posture), then it will be tainted by competitive one-upmanship in which someone is inevitably put down. Often, the insistence that an individual is expressing his or her "authenticity" or "truth" is just another way of claiming to be more important or more righteous than others.

The first time I visited the Esalen Institute, the famed American center for the international human potential movement in Big Sur, California, I had the good fortune of having breakfast with the co-founder, Michael Murphy. Esalen was founded in the early 1960s, and at the height of the Cold War in the 1980s it became known for its focus on citizen-to-citizen diplomacy between the USSR and the US. Murphy and his wife, Dulce, were doing groundbreaking work that led to an ongoing interfaith conversation in the decades to follow, and I had been invited to participate. That commitment to courageous conversation evolved into pioneering work for the global interreligious movement. Talk about using your words instead of violence!

After others finished their breakfast, I talked with Michael Murphy alone. The building we were in hangs off the side of a cliff overlooking the Pacific Ocean, and as we talked over coffee we could see the cargo ships in the distance leaving long silver wakes on the deep-blue waters. The ever-curious Murphy asked about the book I was writing. In my explanation, I used the phrase "authentic self" to describe the result of living free of fear's energy field.

"Oh, beware of that 'authenticity' business," Murphy said right away.

I was very curious to hear what he meant. "Tell me more," I said.

"Authenticity can cover over all sorts of sins," he explained. He recounted a cautionary tale about the dysfunctional use of the term *authenticity*, which I'm calling *false authenticity*. He explained that much damage can be done in the name of an ideological attachment to authenticity. "You have to be careful about the fact that behind all truth claims there can be power grabs."

I nodded in recognition on two levels: the idea of "truth claims" and also "power grabs." As we've seen in the Habit of Truth, contrary to what many people believe there is no one ultimate dogmatic "truth" and Truth itself is not static; the concept of authenticity, as Murphy explained, is similar. Also, throughout my private life and in my career I have had to deal with organized religion hiding behind certain truth claims while concurrently indulging in "power grabs." I instantly recognized the wisdom of his words and saw how a claim of authenticity is used in all sorts of situations as justification for unnecessarily hurtful behavior.

This is true in our personal relationships too. Love-based Candor does not come from one individual seeking power over another or others—this is the fruit of fear-based behavior. "My father didn't like me," my dear friend Jim once told me. "He was always belittling me in front of others, even setting me up for failure. I couldn't understand why he would want to hurt me like that." Tragically, he believed that his father disapproved of his very existence.

Jim's father was born in a small village in Eastern Europe during World War II. As a child, he had lived in a constant state of upheaval and fear. Finally making it to America as a teenager, he settled down with a fellow immigrant in the New York area. Seeing his son experience freedoms he himself had never known brought terror to the heart of this man. He was afraid Jim would get into drugs, get hurt, make bad decisions. It was a struggle reconciling his experiences growing up with the reality of the culture in which Jim was thriving. His father reacted to this fear by saying demeaning things to his son and others; he justified this traumatizing behavior by insisting on the correctness of his worldview—the "authenticity" of his position. In desperately seeking power over his child, he was inadvertently pushing him further and further away. But we see from the way he attempted to express Candor that when it is motivated by fear, it risks being destructive and hurtful rather than empowering.

The complex, multigenerational relationship between parent and child is more vulnerable than any other to the misuse of Candor, as the child fears, more than anything in the world, the loss of that bond. The stakes are enormous. In no other relationship do we have this kind of power imbalance, nor are we as unprepared for abusive attacks that can occur physically, sexually, or emotionally. Trying to bring someone else down, dishonoring another human being, discounting someone else's feelings, or imposing your doctrines on someone are not expressions of Candor. Cruelty is a habit of fear, not love.

Rather, there is a way to exercise Candor in which both parties feel a surge of newness and even transcendence: as we come to experience the Beloved inside ourselves, we also become conscious of the presence of the Beloved in every other person, and in every relationship. This father's Candor could have transformed his relationship with Jim in countless positive ways had it emerged from his loving self rather than his fearful self. Instead, he transmitted his fear and censure to his son, undermining rather than helping him.

When Our *Being* Is Called into Question

It's quite easy to misuse or misunderstand Candor. Under the guise of giving advice, speaking "authentically" from the heart, or sharing an important Truth, blunt words are not Candor at all. When such efforts mask envy, self-righteousness, anger, and fear, Candor has become cruelty. When Michael Murphy and I talked about the abuse of authenticity, something from my memory bank began to resonate; I had a recollection from my teenage years that I had not thought about in decades. The first time I spent a significant time away from home was in 1964 when I was 16 years old. I had been chosen to participate in the summer-long Governor's Honors

Program at Wesleyan College in steamy Macon, Georgia. Four hundred high school students from across Georgia were selected to come together for eight weeks of intensive education in a variety of academic fields and the arts. We were exposed to the brightest and best teachers in all those fields, as well as intelligent and stimulating young counselors who oversaw our dormitories and extracurricular activities.

A few days after arriving in Macon, I settled down onto the grass under the shade of a giant oak along with a group of peers and one of those counselors for one of our very first meetings. Though they seemed so much older than we were, those young college graduates had only five or six years more life experience than we did. In turn, we all introduced ourselves. After I talked, our group leader said, "Ed, you must be a firstborn." I concurred. "I bet your younger sibling, or siblings, came along a little later—leaving you some time as an only child."

"Amazing!" I said, eyes wide. I was excited by his insight. "How did you know?"

"Well, it's obvious, isn't it? You're so narcissistic and controlling, you had to be an only child."

I recoiled in embarrassment. It took me two or three weeks before I was able to open up in group sessions again. This was my first experience with the cruelty of "I'm just being authentic with you" behavior. Let's put to the side for now the fact that I can quite easily match anyone's narcissism and control issues. The point is that this counselor was engaging in a cruel power play in order to show off his expertise in the area of birth order and make an uninvited critique of me—at the level of my personhood—in front of my peers. A much more loving tack would have been to take me aside one afternoon to say something like, "Ed, when you make everything else in the universe about you, that's called narcissism. You might want to try considering that when someone else is having a bad day, it's not your fault, nor is it your responsibility to control them."

There is often confusion between criticism of our doing (our actions) and of our being (our personhood). This confusion contaminates our feeling and thinking. Without knowing how to sort out these feelings and thoughts, we fall prey to taking criticism personally and we deprive ourselves of confidently facilitating candid conversations in our personal and public lives. Think of Gus and Mary, and how deftly—though not easily—he avoided cruelty. Instead of attacking Mary's personhood, he revealed to her that her actions were sometimes difficult for others to handle. This ended up being a gift. Without this kind of Candor we rob ourselves of the personal growth and the richness of relationships that flow from this marvelously freeing and empowering habit.

This dynamic is also at play in the most quotidian circumstances, with our acquaintances, friends, and co-workers. Sometimes we employ Candor unknowingly, and it invariably enriches us and others. A young mother sat by the swings at the playground, her head bent over a book. Her two children were screeching happily as they pumped their legs up and down on the swing set. The older child, Nick, a towheaded boy of about six wearing a silky green soccer uniform, seemed especially boisterous. Families milled around, unpacking picnics of peanut butter sandwiches and sliced apples for their children. A woman approached the young mom and then hesitated.

"Excuse me," she said, her face pinched. "Can I talk to you, Clare?"

Clare looked up and smiled, holding her place in the book with one finger. "Sure. How are you? What's up?"

The smile on Clare's face derailed Olivia. She had been meaning to tell her friend that she'd had it with Nick's behavior. For weeks, mostly in the cafeteria at lunch, Nick had been picking on her son Patrick. She had wanted to say, "I don't know what's going on in your household, but you have to get a grip on your children! It's really out of control. He's such a bully. We—I just can't take it anymore."

Instead, she sat down on the bench next to Clare. She asked her about how things were going at home with the divorce and the custody issues. As she watched the kids playing, she listened quietly. Instantly, Clare began opening up: things were hard, but they were slowly getting better. Olivia invited her for coffee the next day, at which point she would broach the topic of Nick's behavior.

Had Olivia decided to vent her feelings, Clare would have heard this: *You're a bad mother; your son is a bad egg; you've messed up your family.* Instead of being able to accept the Truth of what her friend told her, she would have felt a barrier rising inside her, making it more difficult for them to get to the root of Nick and Patrick's problems and work out a solution. She would have reacted to fear and anger with her own fear and anger. After they had coffee, and Olivia explained what was happening in school, she and Clare were able to become allies instead of enemies.

To practice Candor successfully, we must avoid at all costs criticizing someone's being and pushing him or her into a fear-fueled defensive posture. Talking in private, and prefacing her comments about Nick with an invitation to Clare to become part of the solution, helped Clare see her friend's Candor as positive rather than negative. Since her intent was to solve this problem together rather than to judge or belittle, her approach was one of honesty combined with tact.

Candor Helps You Go Beyond the Surface

One of my colleagues, Theodora, is a stellar example of how powerful the use of Candor can be to free a relationship from the grip of fear and to establish it more in love. Through her own journey she has discovered that lying at the very center of the transformative power of Candor is the identification of feelings—especially the uncomfortable or even painful ones we experience when we are triggered by what another person has said. When these feelings build to a point where we have difficulty communicating with that individual, or we can no longer speak well of this person to others, we may be called upon to have a courageous conversation that digs beneath the surface behavior and into the issue in order to find the root of the problem.

After experiencing the pain of divorce, Theodora fell in love again in late middle age and took the plunge back into marriage with a man named Clarke. But this time they vowed it would be different. They would not let unprocessed negative emotions unravel their relationship. This meant allowing themselves to be vulnerable and forcing themselves to be courageous in their interactions, even about seemingly mundane disagreements.

Some time ago, they were sitting together in Theodora's home in Pasadena enjoying a pasta dinner. Theodora mentioned a holiday party they had been invited to that she was excited about. But Clarke immediately put up roadblocks: he couldn't attend, he said—it was logistically just too complicated and tiring. He would have to drive down from his house in the Bay Area, then return north to celebrate Christmas with his sons, then drive down once again to celebrate Theodora's birthday and Christmas. He encouraged her to go by herself.

"By the time dinner was over," Theodora explained, "I was totally exhausted, sad, depressed—feeling that some elevator inside me had plunged free-fall a hundred floors to my basement—and I had to go upstairs and lie down. I knew it couldn't be just the issue of the party." Half an hour later, she went back downstairs and began to talk candidly with Clarke to expose and then exorcise the painful truths that lay underneath the simple question of attending the party. As they unpacked it all, they talked about feelings.

There was a pervasive sense of sadness about the difficulties they had sharing family time together. No one was to blame, but the sadness was not to be ignored. They would be spending a lot of time apart. This in turn led to feelings of fear of abandonment: Clarke's pacemaker/defibrillator had been going off randomly, and that was terrifying for Theodora. In talking, they realized that while Theodora was indeed perfectly capable of attending that party by herself, the idea of doing so put her in touch with the possibility of being single again, this time as a widow.

Candor is a great compliment to pay to another; it means you are engaging in a risk-filled act while protecting the other person, yourself, and the relationship from the deterioration that happens when we allow fear to claim us instead of love. The practice of Candor actually is an act of care—care of self, care of others, and care of the relationship. Candor also is an act of love and faith—faith that this relationship that is now troubled can have even firmer footing, and faith that on the other side of the risky conversation of Candor is a richer, more profound, and more durable relationship that can endure all sorts of challenges.

Candor is a way of storm-proofing a relationship. As I was completing this book, Clarke died of congestive heart failure. I visited him and Theodora the evening before his defibrillator was disabled. He spoke of the "deep love" he and Theodora shared. That deep love created a peaceful and comforting environment in which they could face his passing. Before I prayed with Clarke and blessed him—and he in turn blessed me—he said, "That deep love, it helped me clean up all my relationships, so when I die tomorrow I will die with peace." The Habit of Candor played a transformative, breakthrough role in helping this couple evolve to a state of equilibrium from which they could then take their next steps in love rather than fear.

When You Need a Helping Hand

Candor in professional situations can be especially tricky. When two parties disagree or clash, sometimes the feelings that are provoked are highly personal. Yet at work we are, quite naturally, uncomfortable being too emotional; feelings sometimes do not serve us well and are hard to parlay into something productive. Instead, we need to find ways to be honest and forthright while remaining professional and constructive.

Sometimes a third party who is less attached to outcomes is needed to defuse the tension and create an opportunity for dialogue that is not so loaded. I have a friend, George, who works at a nonprofit arts center on the East Coast. The mission of his organization includes a commitment to having a staff composed of professionals representing differences in identity and culture. As a consequence, the staff of more than 60 has a mix of personal histories and values. But as George explained, like any large and diverse group, they are not always one happy family. When faced with strife, they have to work especially hard to find constructive ways to communicate and be sensitive to their different backgrounds and work styles.

Some years ago a member of George's staff revealed privileged information to one of the art center's major donors about a former employee who had been fired. Other colleagues were tangentially involved as they knew about—and in one case, contributed to—the breach of confidence. There was an immediate rupture in the tissue of trust necessary for staff cohesion. After such a violation it can take a long time to restore trust, and sometimes that trust is never regained. If a law has been broken, the Habit of Candor may not be necessary, as the issue is acted upon in a predetermined manner according to the rules of the organization. But in George's case, as with many other businesses, there may be infractions and misunderstandings that require all the parties to dissect what happened and its consequences. Here, Candor allows those involved to express their feelings, call for accountability, and explore what kinds of assurances are needed to move forward.

This breach of confidentiality negatively impacted six people on George's staff. The feelings were so deep, they asked a board member, Susannah, to attend the discussion. She acted, in effect, as a mediator to guide the exercise in Candor. They all gathered together in one of their conference rooms and each person articulated his or her version of the issue.

Susannah listened and then took a deep breath. "While I am helping you with this conversation," she said, looking earnestly at each of those present, "I would like you all to be wishing me God-speed and sending me good thoughts."

Quite suddenly, they all wanted more than ever to do the work of Candor required by this problematic situation. The request for goodwill was an acknowledgment that Candor is oftentimes precarious, arduous, artful, and spiritual work. George has since told me that they are still in the process of moving toward a place of restored trust. However, this diverse group of people are able to work together daily without being distracted and confused by overwhelming feelings, and by sharing a committed desire to work it through to a positive outcome. Without that candid conversation and the help of an uninvolved party to alleviate the tension, they would be closer to the wound than to the healing.

At All Saints, we have been practicing similar types of courageous conversations intentionally for a decade. We by no means have reached perfection in this nor in any other area. Our motto is "Progress not Perfection." We remind one another of this value repeatedly. There are times when you might feel that Candor has failed or backfired. In these instances it is important to remember that the Habit of Candor is a process—a way of life—not an end point.

Conversations from the Heart

Sometimes Candor pays a surprise visit in the midst of a conversation where there had been no intention to do anything but make small talk. One day, our daughter and I were sitting on our living room sofa engaged in light banter. A freshman in high school, Alice had recently had her braces taken off. It was wonderful to see her bright, unobstructed smile. We chatted for a while, and then, out of the blue, she announced that she was no longer going to attend church because it made no sense to her anymore.

On one level, I knew this was utterly appropriate developmentally and I did not really have a retort. Yet I felt something calling to go beneath the everyday. And I certainly wanted her to continue going to church. I probed to learn what else was going on but I got nowhere.

"It just doesn't make sense to me, and I'm not going anymore," she repeated, tucking her long blond hair behind her ears. She would not meet my eyes.

I tried many different arguments on her; as I heard my own words I could tell they were intellectual and unpersuasive. I paused. This was not about rational arguments or logic, it was really about my willingness to be vulnerable in front of my daughter.

"Allie," I said, "the real reason I want you to go to church is because I really think we do better as a family during the week if we've been together in church on Sunday."

"But you don't even sit with us!" she responded, still defensive. "You're up there conducting the services and we're sitting all over the church—me with my friends, Peter with his friends, Mom in the choir. We're not even together!"

I grabbed the opportunity I saw and let the Habit of Candor pull me to a place of more self-disclosure. "I know, but I actually can feel you and Peter and Mom in the room. It gives me energy when I look at you. I love the fact that we're around the Eucharistic Table together. I really think we connect in deep ways that I just can't explain."

There was silence.

"Okay," she said finally. And that was it. She continued attending church weekly and she and her family attend weekly worship together pretty regularly now.

The point of this story is not how to get your children to attend worship. Nor is it about family religious traditions. It is about the power of Candor to lead us deeper than our fears. Our unthinking default answers carry no power to create meaningful relationships. The Beloved working through the Habit of Candor leads us not only to use our words, but to use words beyond the level of cliché, words that reveal the part of our being that wants and needs to connect with others, especially those we love. Candor is a conscious exercise — as when Olivia waited to talk with her friend about Nick's behavior. Candor also opens us to consider first, before we speak, that what we are saying may stem from our own insecurities and unsolved mysteries, as Theodora did when talking with Clarke about their time together as a family.

We all have the strength within us to engage in courageous conversations. Courage comes from the French word for heart, *coeur*. Courageous conversations are indeed conversations of the heart. They have a great deal of heart in them even if the person who initiates the Candor isn't conscious of it. When we open ourselves up to the possibility of Candor, we see opportunities to express it and enrich our relationships in our everyday lives.

How to Practice Candor

The image of a scavenger hunt helps me on my journey toward living the Habit of Candor. In a scavenger hunt, you must physically visit a certain place in order to get the clue for where to go next; then you go to that place to retrieve the next clue, and on and on. I once participated in an amusing scavenger hunt for a friend's birthday party. In order to learn where the party was, we had to go to several venues, experience what was in store for us there, find the clue, and repeat that pattern over and over again until we all convened at the party site along with the honoree.

Every major conversation of Candor gives me significant clues for where I need to go in my life for self-improvement, for attaining my goals, for mid-course correction of the goals I have for my life, for being more of a responsible grown-up, for staying on course. In using Candor, we should exercise the same degree of care with strangers and enemies as with our intimate partners. With intimate partners our marriages or life commitments are at stake—with strangers, adversaries, and enemies, the peace quotient in the world is at stake. Every time any one of us practices the Habit of Candor, even in the most pedestrian-appearing encounter, we have made a significant contribution to peace on this planet. That is how momentous Candor is: it is what the world aches for, but it is not easy.

In preparing to exercise the Habit of Candor, ask yourself some threshold questions. "In what relationships am I walking on eggshells?" and "Are there friends, family, and associates with whom I am avoiding contact?" Those are the relationships inviting you to practice love and not fear. Each one of those relationships can receive some degree of healing and maybe even full restoration by exercising the face of love called Candor.

Before engaging in Candor with another human being, always try to achieve your unique form of coming to Stillness. Remember that Stillness has the strength to take us to that emotional place, that inner sanctuary, deeper than the turmoil stirring the waters at the surface. In the state of mind given to us in Stillness, we can access our true self within. Simultaneously we become conscious of the true self in others. In Stillness we intuitively distinguish between the states of being and doing in ourselves and in others, thereby avoiding the cruelty of attacking, dishonoring, and even wounding someone's being.

Be clear about your motives. Are your goals to be constructive and achieve positive change, or are they motivated by anger—the desire for power or revenge? It is fortifying to imagine how you want to be feeling and thinking afterward and what shape you want your relationship to be in after this risk-filled act of respect. When you realistically imagine the aftermath of the candid truths you plan to share, often you will realize that you *must* present your truths lovingly, otherwise the result risks being horrible, and the whole attempt will end up destructive rather than constructive. Before exercising Candor, I go to Stillness. Then I imagine my desired outcome being a deepened, more durable relationship. I remember how much I respect the other person on the level of being and that I want to confine any critical comments to the area of doing. I'm amazed at how effectively this process helps me succeed in the courageous conversation.

Identify the *being* part of the other person you can celebrate as well as the other *doing* parts of their lives you appreciate. Make a list and spend some time in Stillness appreciating these qualities. It is infinitely easier to share criticisms of behavior after you secure a foundation of affirmation. You will draw on these observations during your conversation.

Be aware, too, that there are persons with whom you may not be able to have a successful candid conversation, as was the case with Rachel and her mother. That is a sad reality of human existence. Candor cannot be coercive; it can only be loving if you are unattached to the results. Sometimes in the exercise of Candor we discover that there is actually an occasion to forgive. Living in the spirit of Candor is an ongoing endeavor that does not always have tidy outcomes.

Of all the habits, Candor is the riskiest as it involves another person toward whom we must act responsibly. Because of this we must lay the groundwork carefully. Ask the other person if he or she has the time and is in a mental state to engage in a candid conversation. If the answer is no, wait for another opportunity. If the answer is yes, proceed with some clear and kind expression of the importance of the person and the issue involved. Spend time simply expressing positive things about the other person on both the being and the doing level. Often I have said to Hope or to a friend or colleague, "I want you to know how valuable our relationship is to me. I don't want to do anything or say anything that will impair our relationship and the flow of life between us. So, are you in a place where we can revisit and discuss the time I think I may have hurt you [or the time when I got my feelings hurt]?" This is also of critical importance when dealing with professional relationships. Invoking how important the affiliation is and then asking if the other person is in a place and has the time to do this demanding work are two crucial strategies to use in Candor. You may be undertaking a risky endeavor, but it has the potential to have an immensely positive outcome.

When you state the issue, describe the impact on you, others, and the project involved. Oftentimes a conversation of Candor involves sorting through feelings as Theodora did with her husband. Consider these questions: Have I respectfully heard the other person's side of the story? Have we both accounted for behavior that was damaging? Do I know and feel that the other person's being and future is more important than this one instance? Ideally, you will want to experience some sense of the Beloved in three ways: within yourself, within the other, and between each of you. That stated desire and the energy of that intention are powerful enough to be manifested in reality. But also acknowledge that sometimes these ideals are just not entirely feasible. Candor calls for patience and persistence over time.

It is crucial that you allow time for the other person to respond to what you have said. I try to keep in mind that despite my best intentions, my efforts may have a very different impact than I'd hoped for. The exchange must feel like an honest mutual exchange, not a unilateral barrage of criticism. Just as you are seeking an opportunity to speak with Candor, you must allow for the person or persons with whom you have a disagreement to respond in kind. Ideally, everyone should have a few moments to talk without interruption. Then, if at all possible, let the ensuing conversation unfold over time, perhaps even putting it on hold until some hours or days have passed.

Stay confident and in your Stillness. Avoid being defensive. You are not alone; the Beloved is working with all of us to bend the history of the human family toward the Habits of Love. You have thought this through and your intention is kind. To remain true to your loved and loving self, do your best and acknowledge that you have tried. Everything else is in the hands of the Beloved.

CHAPTER FIVE

The Habit of Play

Men are born soft and supple;
Dead, they are stiff and hard.
Plants are born tender and pliant;
Dead, they are brittle and dry.

Thus whoever is stiff and inflexible
Is a disciple of death.
Whoever is soft and yielding
Is a disciple of life.

—Lao-tzu

Unless you change
and become like little children,
you will never enter the kingdom of heaven.

—Jesus (Matthew 18:3, NRSV)

The Dalai Lama was giving a lecture to an audience of hundreds when, deeply engaged in a discussion on compassion, it occurred to him to illustrate his point with a rather elongated story. At the end of the story the Dalai Lama fell quiet. Sitting among the crowd, I waited for him to complete his thought, but he remained silent.

For a long, long time.

After a while, we all began to shift in our seats, uncomfortable with the extended pause. Then, the Dalai Lama's dark eyebrows shot upward, his face creased, and he began to laugh. His laughter devolved into giggles. It was utterly infectious; soon the crowd was laughing too.

"I forgot the point I was making in my lecture," His Holiness said finally, once the first wave of laughter rippling through the crowd subsided.

We all erupted into laughter again. The Dalai Lama's self-awareness, combined with his willingness to laugh at himself, showed us all just how freeing it is to operate from our open-hearted selves, using humor and humility, instead of from our fearful selves. When we take ourselves too seriously, it is because we are afraid of failing to measure up to expectations—our own and others'. Undesirable thoughts begin to multiply: *I'm afraid that I'm not going to get it right and that not getting it right will be catastrophic. I'm afraid that I will be mistaken. I'm afraid I won't be taken seriously.* The Dalai Lama had no fear of not being taken seriously.

While each of the Habits of Love invites earnest engagement, Play asks us to distinguish between this earnestness and a deadly seriousness that tricks us into thinking that our specific concern is the only urgent one in the entire universe. In taking ourselves too seriously, we lose the perspective necessary for creative problem solving. We lose awareness of any other interests but the one that is making us fearful. This is the very essence of the fearful self. When we operate out of love, on the other hand, we can invite Play into our lives more readily and benefit from the spirit of lightheartedness and flexibility it introduces.

The Habit of Play literally changes our brain chemistry, freeing us to access our imaginations, and to become the most creative, constructive, and joyful individual we can be. Play and its benefits are some of the most loving gifts we can give ourselves and others. A dance teacher once told her class, "Dancers, I want you to dance now, but not the way fear makes you dance." Let's dance now through the Habit of Play.

The Wonder of the Child

When people become too uptight, we often speak of "kidding" them into a more playful space. That turn of phrase is no accident: when we're too serious minded we need to become more like a kid. Play returns us to our loving selves by awakening our sense of childlikeness, which is marked by joy, freshness, imagination, and movement. Here we make an important distinction, of course, between play-oriented *childlikeness*—being reacquainted with rhythm, laughter, imagination, and wonder—and *childishness*, which is defined by an inability to take responsibility and to see unselfishly beyond our needs alone.

When Jesus said that we cannot enter the kingdom of heaven unless we change and become like little children, he was referring to this notion of childlikeness. His metaphor, the "kingdom of heaven," refers to a state of spiritual and mental being in this life on earth; children are the essential role models of this concept. Children have an exquisite capacity to play, to imagine, to create stories, to connect with nature, art, and ritual. When children move into an imaginative space in their minds and spirits, a world of possibility and promise opens up for everyone.

One fall morning my four-year-old grandson, Luke, was getting into the car with his mother for the ride to his preschool. As my daughter was buckling him into his car seat, Luke squirmed and said, "Mommy, it's going to be a great day for us!"

"Why, sweetie?" Alice asked.

"Well, Mommy!" he said, his face beaming with the discovery of something extraordinary. "Look at the pretty trees!"

Whenever I think of Luke's forecast based on the beauty of the multihued autumn trees, I automatically smile and take a deep breath. Play takes place in me just as it took place in him that morning. My heart feels lighter and more open to a day full of possibility. The distinction between childlikeness and childishness is that childlikeness makes room for *everyone* to play: "Mommy, it's going to be a great day for *us*."

In contrast, when we behave childishly we can only be aware of our own concerns and narrowed perspectives. I once briefly attended a church dinner celebrating the bishop's annual visit to All Saints. That night I felt nauseous and lightheaded, and I suspected I was coming down with the flu. Though I knew I needed to be in bed, I stopped by the crowded dining hall to welcome the bishop before regretfully heading home. The following week, I received a single-spaced typed letter from one of my parishioners named Steve. He announced that he was leaving the church because "it is obvious that you don't care anything about me."

Steve had been offended by my quick departure. He took my behavior as a personal slight and became so upset that he left the church. I wrote him a note explaining what had happened from my perspective and told him as lovingly as I could that I would personally keep his pew warm and available when he was ready to return. Three years later he did return, and now he never misses a Sunday. Every time I'm with him I try to kid him into a less childish and a more childlike frame of mind.

Through Play we become more creative; we feel refreshed rather than staid; others relate to us more easily; our perspectives are deepened. Oftentimes allowing the child within to burst free is a powerful antidote to a sobering reality. When I invite Play into my life, I am better able to help others. I am better at problem solving and thinking both independently and inventively. Play enables me to live with Luke's childlike optimism and munificence. It opens both my heart and my mind.

Allowing Slack in the Line

The Habit of Play allows us to step back from the ever-present anxiety that gnaws at us, wears us down, and can lead us to make poor decisions that are based on fear. My mentor, Rabbi Ed Friedman, often used the image of a person fishing to describe the interplay of competing forces in our lives, our families, and our institutions. A person who is good at fishing makes certain that there is always "play" in the line. If the line is too tight it is difficult to gauge whether you have a bite. However, if you have some play in your line, you can feel immediately whether there is a bite and you can respond appropriately.

One of Friedman's favorite stories was about his son, and it illustrates this point perfectly. When he was still a teenager, his son was involved in a minor automobile accident in which he rear-ended a woman's car as she was driving to work. No one was hurt, and even though it was his first accident, the boy was summoned to appear in traffic court.

When father and son arrived at court, the other driver was pacing the room, her face reddened; she wanted to throw the book at the boy. As the legal points were batted back and forth, Rabbi Friedman began to sense that the judge and lawyers were getting caught up in the plaintiff's escalating intensity and emotion. He actually felt the force field of anxiety building around the judge's bench and the adjacent area. Anxiety and fear can create their own force fields, which can be sensed quite tangibly. As the level of fear continued to rise, the rabbi realized that he too was getting tight and was losing his perspective to the power of fear. His heart started beating fast, and he began to sweat; he was getting angrier and angrier. His son looked at him with pleading eyes. Everything seemed to be getting out of control. The rising panic was infectious and debilitating.

Friedman decided to move away from the others to the back of the courtroom, out of the web of anxiety that the reactive person had inadvertently spun. Removing himself from the action, he slowly came to feel centered again and the Habit of Play shone its light on him.

Returning to the front of the courtroom, the judge asked him what he, the father, thought the appropriate punishment was.

"Life imprisonment!" he replied, with a smile on his lips. "This is surely the worst crime a young man can commit—to have a fender bender against this woman."

The judge and lawyers started laughing. After just a beat, the plaintiff's face softened visibly and she laughed too. Perspective was regained. The matter was resolved without resorting to extreme measures and everyone went home.

By practicing the Habit of Play, the rabbi helped everyone back away from the precipice of overprosecuting a young man for a minor mistake. Fear often registers in our bodies and moods as being tense. You know how it is difficult to dance with someone who is uptight? You have to be able to "feel" your dance partner in order to sense the next moves on the dance floor. If your body is too tight and controlling, it is impossible to respond to your partner, much less the rhythm of the music. In the same way, anxiety keeps us from moving to life's rhythms and blocks us from accessing our loving selves. Play's childlike essence helps us connect with our inner sanctuary, and so guides us away from making poor decisions that are motivated by our fears.

Ed Friedman maintained an often subversive, jesterlike spirit, all the while keeping "play" in his fisherman's line. His calling was to cheer on the persons in the family or institutions who were moving toward greater health. Of course, he couldn't identify or encourage this energy in others if he himself was too tight, too serious, or too vulnerable to chronic anxiety. Our fearful selves render us insensitive to others around us; unwittingly, we become egocentric. In the years I knew him, Friedman reminded me again and again of the healing power of Play and its astonishing ability to bridge the gaps that can open up between us.

When Play Infuses All We Do

The Habit of Play is not a frivolous activity to be engaged in only during our "spare time." Its benefits are crucial to congregations, companies, or Congress, and to living our lives fully and well; it does not belong relegated to the sidelines.

We need only look to today's most inventive and successful companies to see an argument for embracing Play in all areas of our lives. With the rise of technology, particularly the Internet and the personal computer, came the understanding that actively promoting creativity and imagination in the work world was often a key to greater business success—and also to improved employee satisfaction. Employers began encouraging the spirit of Play.

In certain sectors of the business world there is a marked appreciation of the essential role of Play in accomplishing the goal of creative productivity. I remember seeing for the first time a picture of Internet-startup Google's office space in Mountain View, California. It included Ping-Pong tables in the communal areas and undulating, brightly colored walls to the offices. Soon other young companies followed suit, incorporating Play into their workspace and into their workday. It is not unusual to see team members engaging in a heated game of beach volleyball outside Oracle's headquarters in San Francisco. In a small business in downtown Boston, co-workers gather throughout the day to celebrate Red Sox victories or birthdays. Arcade games and dartboards have made their way into cafeteria areas. The online retailer Zappos, based in southern Las Vegas, encourages costume parties and parades at its headquarters.

When we invite Play into all areas of our lives, we turn away from our fearful natures and invite the loving self to reengage with the world and with the parts of our brains that imagine and create. It makes us better employees and employers, better friends, partners, and parents. Research shows that it's hard to be an effective and supportive leader when the institution or family we are part of is op-

erating from a state of fear or anxiety. We can see this happening
in our modern political culture, when fear crowds out playfulness.
The American political system wears down leaders by sabotaging
their visionary thinking with constant, predictable, partisan reac-
tions, rather than thoughtful responses. Just take the discussion that
takes place every August, when many passionately debate whether
the US president should or should not go on vacation. Usually
the strongest hue and cry comes from the opposition party, whose
personal reactive interests lie in rendering the opposition leader
ineffective. This is, of course, what happens when no distance is
gained on the angst and power grabs swirling in Washington, D.C.,
and the wider world.

Contrary to what some people believe, Play does not detract
from our responsibilities or obfuscate our eventual objectives. It is
not an excuse for being childish or irresponsible. Rather, the Habit
of Play celebrates the humanity and creativity in each of us and
encourages us to explore further and dig deeper, making us more
resilient and less egocentric. It helps us find unconventional, even
adventurous, solutions to problems that may otherwise appear intractable.

A Release from Fear and Illness

Being playful not only helps us in the moment by relieving tension,
opening our hearts, and returning the blood supply to our higher
brain functions, but it also sets us up to be more successful and
healthier as we continue our journey through life. My friend Stuart
tells the story of "busking" with his daughter when she was seven
and eight years old. Busking, loosely defined, is playing music on
the street for money. Together they learned the entire *Sgt. Pepper's
Lonely Hearts Club Band* album by the Beatles and performed
in parks and on street corners, father playing guitar and daughter
singing.

"Some dads take their kids fishing," his wife said by way of explanation, with a shrug and a smile.

Sometimes when they were in the car on their way to their impromptu gigs, Stuart or his daughter might start to feel tightness or anxiety. One of them would ask, "Why are we doing this again?"

"To face our fears!" the other one would answer.

The experience of setting up musical instruments in front of unsuspecting passersby has helped Stuart's daughter go on to accomplish other things that likewise required stepping into the void, when she did not know exactly what was going to happen next. In an uncertain world, Play helps us find the courage to take risks. It helps us weather disappointments and withstand pain. It even makes us more resilient to stresses that can profoundly impact our mental and physical well being.

Dr. Esther Sternberg knows a great deal about anxiety's magnetic field, both from professional and personal experience; she has become an internationally recognized leader in researching the mind-body connection. Earlier in her career, when Dr. Sternberg's mother was dying of cancer, she frequently flew from Maryland to Montreal and back again. As a result of the tension of that fraught travel and the stresses of the grieving process, she developed inflammatory arthritis.

Spiritually depleted and physically drained, Sternberg's playful nature was completely buried by her grief and exhaustion. Though as a scientist she knew that inherited genes play an important role in causing disease, she also understood that the reason illness strikes at a particular moment is often due more to fear and anxiety than to a simple accident of fate. "I believe there's no question and there's evidence to support the notion," she wrote, "that being chronically stressed can be associated with triggering these sorts of diseases from burnout."

It was not until she took a trip to the Greek island of Crete and visited the site of the ancient temple of Asclepius—the Greek god of healing—that she reached her own turning point. Looking over the parched landscape and the ruins shimmering in the heat, she finally viscerally understood that she could not be whole and healthy unless she found a way to rejuvenate her spirit. "We take our cars in to be serviced every five thousand miles, but we don't do that for ourselves," she wrote. "Any amount of time that you can devote to going off-line, in whatever way you find, will help."

Many of us have been in similar situations during which we finally come to realize how deeply connected mind and body are. I know a young man named Harold whose wife gave birth to twin boys a few years ago. Harold is a currency trader who sits for long hours in front of a computer. He met his wife, Gale, in college playing varsity tennis, but they no longer had much free time to slam the balls back and forth on the tennis courts. When the twins were six months old, Harold began experiencing pain in his neck and upper back. Even when he was exhausted, he found he could not fall asleep again after being awakened in the night by one of the boys. His mood became dark, and his colleagues started avoiding him at work. Though Gale needed time off for herself too, she could tell that Harold was suffering physically and she urged him to see a doctor.

Because his back troubles affected his ability to do his work, Harold eventually committed to going regularly to a physical therapist. They often talked, and the therapist became interested in Harold's stories about playing college tennis.

"Well, I certainly don't have time for *that* anymore," Harold complained.

The therapist laughed as he dug his thumbs into his patient's rotator cuff. He suggested Harold take up badminton instead.

Explaining to me the genius of this simple idea, Harold's face became animated. "I didn't have the energy to be competitive anymore," he said. "But he was right that I needed a break—something fun and physical that I could do with Gale." He bought a small net and some plastic flyers. The following weekend they played the first of many games of badminton in the park while the children watched from a portable playpen. They don't care about who wins or loses, and much of the time they run around aimlessly, teasing each other and laughing.

"It's just what the doctor ordered," Harold says. "And of course, my backache is much, much better."

Once Dr. Sternberg and Harold were able to embrace a more carefree spirit and revel in the glory of Play, they began to heal emotionally and physically. Harold also saw a marked improvement in his relationship with Gale because he had more patience and empathy. Similarly, when Stuart and his daughter overcame their fear and performed in front of strangers, they were fortifying themselves against potential difficulties the future might hold. The Habit of Play restores us to ourselves in so many profound ways.

Opening the Door to Creativity

When we are strung too tightly, everything seems a chore. Our bodies become depleted, our minds muddled. We are unable to make good decisions, and our imaginative capacity shrivels. Allowing Play into our lives reverses this: our bodies become healed and our minds begin to blossom again. One January morning I was standing in line at a coffee shop deeply preoccupied with my day's agenda. I was not in a playful place, to say the least. My head bent low, I had not noticed the people around me and I am sure they had not given me a second glance. The line moved slowly and irritation mounted inside me. I was certain all these other people could not possibly be as burdened with work as I was.

And then, out of the speakers came the opening measures of a Motown song I had danced to as a teenager. Its irresistible beat instantly permeated the crowded shop. Everything about me changed: I'm sure that the pleasure centers of my brain started firing like mad. Involuntarily, I began to move my body; every muscle became fluid as I danced in place. The intense pleasure of the present moment eclipsed worries about getting everything done today. I asked the tattooed clerk if the store had a CD with the song on it available for purchase.

"No. We just love Marvin Gaye here," he said, grinning at me.

I paid for my coffee, lingered in the coffee shop till the song was over, and then sauntered back to my car, the song beginning the first of many replays in my mind. My spiritual jukebox can still order up that song for an instantaneous smile in my heart and fluidity in my body.

The song is "Stubborn Kind of Fellow," Marvin Gaye's first breakthrough hit recorded in 1962 after three failed singles. Because of the song's hold on me that day, I began to think that there was more going on than a fleeting coffee store moment that had jolted me from preoccupation to Play. A childlike notion began to grow in my mind: Dare I try to give next Sunday's worshippers something of the fun I had tasted in the shop that day?

As I sat in Stillness the following morning, meditating about the sermon, the components of the liturgy began to assume creative roles with one another in my imagination. That next Sunday we would be baptizing children. Could I introduce the spirit of Play into this often rather solemn ritual—and would others be enriched by this experience? I came to realize there were too many prompts to Play in church for me to ignore and I went for it.

That Sunday, I invited all gathered in the church to stand, gave them permission to dance if they felt so moved, and reminded them that the love each of us has comes from a "stubborn kind of lover," as the song puts it—in my own words, from the Beloved. Everyone stood, and as parents brought children forward to be baptized, with a few stiff exceptions, the entire gathering began to move and clap. In some cases, parishioners actually danced at their pew or in the aisles as we played over our loudspeakers the recording of Marvin Gaye with Martha and the Vandellas singing backup:

I'm gonna love you (gonna love you in every way)
in every way (gonna love you in every way)
Ohhhhhhh! I'm gonna love you (gonna love you in every way)
in every way-ay-ay-ay-ay.

I danced from the pulpit to the baptismal font and presided over one of the happiest and most playful baptisms of my life. Infused with the spirit of Play, through the power of music, I was able to make meaningful creative connections I would otherwise have missed—and I could then share that inspiration with others, thereby infinitely multiplying the bounty. This is the power of the Beloved working inside us.

When Play Feels Wrong

For some of us, accessing the spirit of Play can be exceptionally hard. Looking around us, it sometimes seems we are surrounded by too much pain, poverty, illness, and destruction to allow ourselves to be playful. We see political systems that appear to be broken and financial structures that are rotten. Perhaps we have experienced failure or we fear future failures. Perhaps we are serious-minded people and are challenged by lightheartedness. Or perhaps we have lost someone dear to us, and cannot yet move on from that place of sorrow and solitude. But if we can reconnect with the childlike spirit of Play, fighting the impulse to hold every moment in a vise-like grip, we will find our lives enriched in myriad ways.

When we fail to engage in playfulness, we also inadvertently set up barriers between ourselves and those we work with or love. Sean is the youngest brother of a friend of mine and has been an environmentalist for over three decades—long before the movement gained any traction in the consciousness of average folk. For years, instead of feeling that humankind was making progress, Sean felt it was self-destructing. There were entire days when he did not laugh or smile. It did not occur to him to watch a funny movie, play a board game, or gently tease a friend. He industriously tended to his small farm, from which he feeds himself and his family, raising chickens, planting edible gardens, and collecting rainwater for irrigation. From his perspective, there was no point in being playful. It was not practical. It wasted time and denied the reality in which we live. Sean's reluctance to engage in Play—whether because he was unable or unwilling to do so, I'm not entirely sure—interfered with his professional success. Other people found him hard to relate to and felt he was a know-it-all. He became increasingly isolated.

Then five years ago Sean and his girlfriend had a baby girl named Tabitha. Though initially the added responsibility was daunting, the infusion of the baby's childlike spirit into his home pulled Sean inexorably toward the light. He was more tired than ever before, but he also laughed more than ever before. His heart opened to allow in the joy of silliness. Who can look at the antics of a young child they adore and not appreciate the everyday moments that hold within them countless tiny miracles of existence?

It is only human to experience anxiety about our disappointments or sorrows. These difficult feelings reveal that we care deeply about what is happening in the world around us, and make us part of the greater human family. The kind of resilience and suppleness engaged by the Habit of Play is totally compatible with the full range of our human emotions. I'm reminded of my experience in the coffee shop, and the way the music lifted my spirits and invited me to engage in a realm that took me away from my self-absorption and anxiety. When we overcome our reluctance to Play—our instinct to remain so earnest and self-involved—we are able to connect with our loving selves and with others in a way that is truly life affirming. That helps us deal with anger, sadness, and fear without denying that they are a reality.

Through Play we learn patience. We learn to reach out to others. Hope and light will bounce back. We must trust that we are never truly alone, and engaging others in the Habit of Play reminds us of this simple truth.

A Moment of Sorrow Transformed

I can't end a chapter on the Habit of Play without relating one more story about my dear friend Rabbi Friedman. His intuitive sense of Play and his radically inclusive and inquisitive nature had such a powerful influence on me in the many years we worked together.

One Friday morning, the phone in my office rang. It was a friend calling to say that Ed Friedman had suffered a fatal heart attack.

I slumped to the floor weeping. Something more powerful than me had struck me—I was literally "grief stricken." As a colleague said, "It's like we've all of a sudden had the windshield removed in a fast-moving car." I was stunned.

On the eve of the funeral, I arrived frantic and devastated in Bethesda, Maryland, in the late afternoon. Unpacking my bags at the hotel, I discovered something critical was missing. In my haste, I had forgotten my dress shoes; the only ones I had with me were the running shoes I had worn on the plane.

Trying to keep my cool, I hailed a cab and raced to the closest men's store. It was ten minutes to closing time. Out of breath but relieved, I asked the nearest clerk for the kind of shoes I needed in my size.

"I'm so sorry," she said, looking at me sympathetically, "but this store no longer carries shoes."

There was no possible way I could make it to another store before closing time. My cool flew out the window. I called my contact Susan Luff, a member of Ed's faculty, in a state of near panic.

A word about Susan: for ten years, she facilitated small-group meetings during which we reflected on our anxiety levels within our families and other systems in which we interacted. This was part of my research work as a student of Rabbi Friedman's. During that decade, Susan had playfully shed light on my own journey of self-discovery. This night was to be no exception.

"Susan, I don't have any dress shoes for tomorrow!" I blurted out as soon as she picked up.

"What happened?" Susan asked.

"I forgot to pack them. I've raced to the store . . ." As my story unfurled, my throat got tighter, my voice more strident, my tone more desperate.

Then I heard laughing in the background.

"Susan," I barked into the phone, as the doors of the store were being locked behind me. "You're laughing at me!"

Night had fallen. Standing on the street under the lights, I was alone. Rabbi Friedman was dead. My intellectual windshield was gone. I was so uptight at that moment that the most important of all concerns seemed to be my lack of dress shoes to wear the following day. Here I was, a grown-up student of how chronic anxiety can hurt us, reduced to a pity party. I had totally lost perspective.

But at the same time I was forming that indignant response about Susan laughing at me, a mysterious and playful sense of joy was peeking out from behind the curtain of sorrow. All in one moment—what the King James Version of the Bible calls "in the twinkling of an eye" (1 Corinthians 15:52)—I began to see what had happened. I had allowed myself to become morbidly anxious, leading to a childish and egocentric view of the situation.

Now Susan was laughing even harder. She was not being cruel; with every laugh I heard a message: *Can the real Ed Bacon come out to play?*

"Well, I guess you'll have to speak in your running shoes," she finally said. There was a long silence. "You'll be in good company."

This was followed by an even longer silence, interspersed with unsuccessfully suppressed chuckles. "And by the way, we decided to bury Ed in *his* running shoes."

Though Ed Friedman was never unkempt, neither would he have made anyone's best-dressed list. While I was his student, the rabbi made two overnight teaching visits to the cathedral where I was dean. Both times he brought only his attaché case, into which he crammed clean underclothes, toiletries, and tomorrow's fresh shirt. He didn't want the bother of checking or carrying luggage. A sturdy, lovingly worn-in pair of running shoes were always on his feet, whether he was teaching or going for a walk. It was fitting that his family and Susan, who was helping with the funeral, had decided to bury him in those signature running shoes.

Perceiving Susan's unspoken message to lighten up, regain some resilience, and enter into the spirit of the man whose life we were celebrating, I began to laugh too. I remembered the significance of playfulness for Ed Friedman, and with her laughter Susan had helped me excavate my own sense of Play. The next morning, I rose and dressed in a Brooks Brothers tie and gray flannel suit and scuffed green-and-white running shoes. I went to the funeral, strode to the lectern, and told the story of my panic about the shoes. I detailed the mad race to the store, the yelling at Susan, her laughing in my face, my return to the thinking part of my brain, and noted that Ed and I were the only ones wearing running shoes to his funeral. As talismans to Play, I have saved those running shoes to this day.

Ed Friedman's funeral was a magnificent outpouring of poignant memories mixed with a liberal dose of good humor. In a like manner, every one of Jesus's parables ends in a party. Everyone who loses his or her way finds it again. Many of the stories go through touching and painful times. The land of anxiety and shadow are by no means absent. In the end, however, the strongest force in the story is love.

Love always wins. We can bet our lives on it. Play helps us access that loving nature so our own burdens become lighter and we can reach out and connect meaningfully to others.

How to Practice Play

The ability to engage the Habit of Play keeps us fresh, engaged, and open. It does not erode our stature but enhances it. Think of a teacher who mesmerizes a classroom of squirming students with his combination of humor and intellect. The politician who is humanized by laughing at her own silly mistake. The parent who can turn a rebellious child into a fast ally through a well-timed joke, defusing the tension.

Yet Play can be deceptively complicated for some of us. And it's not always evident when Play is called for and when it is inappropriate. But it is indisputable that the spirit of Play gives us a truer and more useful perspective on the world by helping rid us of our tendency to put ourselves at the heart of every equation. In engaging in Play, we are saying, *I am human; I am fallible; we are all in the same boat.*

Most important, Play releases creative forces within us that are otherwise dampened by duties and egocentrism. When we cannot let go of mistakes or see the absurdity of life, we become constrained and uptight. Play helps us keep the distance we need to observe rather than identify with the natural anxieties of life, and reminds us of the innate creativity and love that lies at the core of our loving selves.

❋ Approach life with the spirit of a learner (an idea introduced in the Stillness chapter) and you will engage Play more naturally. When we adopt the learning spirit, we may still have our fears but we do not *become* our fears. We make mistakes but we are not a mistake. After witnessing the Dalai Lama's self-deprecating laughter, my public speaking was transformed. Louis Pasteur once said, "Chance favors a prepared mind," but there is also preparation constructed in the climate of nervousness that is fed by the fear of failure. When I prepare my sermons, I now offer what I know in a learning spirit and am willing, during and after the experience, to learn from my feedback.

Whatever activity you enter into, allow enough slack in your line to learn from your experience.

* Notice and respect what your body is telling you. With this habit, as well as all Habits of Love, it is important to be aware of the quotient of fear and love in your body. Recall some moments when you were being childlike, both when you were a child and when you were an adult. Try to remember how your body felt during those moments. When you feel physically tight, this is an indication that your fearful self is rearing its ugly head. Uptight people can't imagine anything but the "same old, same old." Allow yourself to loosen up, both physically and mentally, and you will be flooded with ideas and energy. Chances are that in Play you can imagine solutions to seemingly intractable problems.

* In a tense situation at work or in a social setting when you don't know others well, it can be hard to tell when Play is appropriate or to know how to engage it. I suggest that if you sense your muscles tightening up, you at least consider introducing an element of Play in order to lift the mood. In so doing, focus on yourself as opposed to anyone else; you might take a deep breath and make light of yourself, for example. Never poke fun at or tell a story about others, as you cannot be sure they will be in the mood to receive your words in the spirit they were intended. But if you keep the emphasis on yourself, you will invite humor without risking offense.

* Though it seems counterintuitive, Play can and should be practiced. Phyllis Diller once came to speak during the adult education hour at All Saints. She kept us all in stitches for 30 minutes and then answered questions. "I've never been funny. I've never been able to tell a joke successfully," said one of the more earnest members of my church. "What would you recommend?" Miss Diller could have made fun of the question and the questioner, but she did not. I was amazed. She knew how important this issue was. "Buy a book of

jokes. Find a few that make you smile, if not laugh," she advised. "Learn one or two jokes and practice them the next time you're in a social situation. *Feel* how good it feels to laugh and to make others laugh. This is very important." The great comics know that practicing up on the Habit of Play is essential.

Spend time with children during which you observe and learn from them rather than the other way around. If the children do not draw you into their play life, ask simple questions that could be your passport to visiting their world of imagination. You might ask: "What do you imagine that horse is thinking about right now? If they could speak, what would those clouds be saying to us? What are those stars and the moon talking about right now?" Any question that invites imagination is game. Isn't that one of the things we do with Play, after all? Play a game?

When you have made an error, acknowledge it with humor. No one is so very important that they cannot make a mistake every now and then. One of my favorite opportunities to use Play is when I say something that is mistaken and I am corrected. For instance, I recently said rather emphatically at a meeting, "We've never discussed that issue at a staff meeting." The youth minister just happened to have the minutes of the November 4 meeting and said, "It shows here that we indeed did discuss that issue—and that you were present." I responded with a lopsided smile, and said immediately, "Like I said, '*We had a thorough discussion of the matter at the November 4 meeting.*'" Everyone laughed and then we carried on. The point is, when you can accept with humility or humor that you make mistakes, you let people know you are human—just like they are.

Consider ways to invite Play into your work life. Could you suggest a dart board in the cafeteria? A night out for your team members? A game of bowling for the support staff? An all-staff night at a karaoke bar? If you can find a way to embrace your Community by laughing together, your daily interactions will be filled with greater joy and more creativity.

If you tend to be a serious type, call to mind those in your life or imagination who have achieved more of a balance between purposeful and functional action on the one hand, and the ability to have restorative fun on the other. Who of your playful friends can call you out to play—both literally and emotionally—when you're being too tight? Intentionally spend more time with those playful friends.

CHAPTER SIX

The Habit of Forgiveness

Last night while I was sleeping
I dreamed, blessed epiphany!
That I had a beehive
Inside my heart;
And the golden bees
Were making
From my old bitternesses
White beeswax and sweet honey.

—Antonio Machado

Shortly after the Apartheid rule in South Africa was ended and Nelson Mandela was inaugurated president of a new nonracial South Africa, he established what was known as the Truth and Reconciliation Commission. It sought to bring light to all the heinous transgressions committed by both sides of the conflict during that bloody period.

The rules were simple: if you gave a full confession acknowledging your guilt to those you harmed, you would not be punished. The underpinning theory was that this fragile new nation could progress toward its destiny of freedom and equality only to the degree that its past received the healing light and balm of both truth and reconciliation. Offering Forgiveness to truth-tellers was the only way forward. As Archbishop Desmond Tutu, the iconic face of this Commission, said in his book: there is *No Future Without Forgiveness.*

One day the Commission brought in an elderly black woman to face the white policeman, Mr. Van de Broek, who had tortured, murdered, and then cremated the lady's son and husband some years earlier. The scope of his depravity extended to forcing this wife and mother to witness his unspeakable crimes against her family members. The last words she heard her husband speak before he finally died were "Father, forgive them."

"How do you believe justice should be done to this man who has inflicted such suffering on you and so brutally destroyed your family?" asked one of the members of the Commission.

She said she wanted Van de Broek to go to the place where they burned her husband's body and gather up the dust so she could give him a decent burial. His head bent low, the policeman nodded agreement. The old woman paused, collecting herself, and then continued. "Mr. Van de Broek took all my family away from me, and I still have a lot of love to give. Twice a month, I would like for him to come to the ghetto and spend a day with me so I can be a mother to him."

But she had one last wish. "I would like Mr. Van de Broek to know that he is forgiven by God, and that I forgive him too." She asked for someone to lead her across the courtroom. "I would like to embrace him so he can know that he is truly forgiven."

When he heard these words, Mr. Van de Broek fainted.

Together, the friends, family, and neighbors gathered in the hearing room—all victims of repression and discrimination—began to sing the hymn "Amazing Grace."

This story always leaves me wanting to take a deep breath and have a moment to pause. This kind of Forgiveness is difficult to fathom, and yet it always remains as a choice for an individual, or a nation, that has been severely wounded. This remarkable mother, who is an exemplar of what it means to be human, made the instinctive connection between Forgiveness and her own desire to live according to her loving self when she said that she wanted the perpetrator to become her son so she could pour her remaining love into him.

To those who have been deeply scarred, this choice may appear outrageous or out of the realm of the possible. But in order to create an interior world of freedom as well as an external world of peace and justice, the Habit of Forgiveness must be engaged.

A Flow of Positive Energy

The only essential to practicing the Habit of Forgiveness is a genuine wish for both yourself and your adversary to become whole. Naturally, there are times when we cannot manage this. But we will see that, in genuinely opening ourselves to the power of Forgiveness, we ourselves become free.

When we experience Forgiveness, it is as though a powerful, loving energy is released and able to move through us. Before we reach Forgiveness, this energy is powerful but can become blocked—it bumps up against obstructions that have been caused by real or imagined hurts. This energy becomes one of pain, sorrow, and confusion and remains trapped in our bodies and minds. But when we are able to forgive, the blockages melt away so that life can flow again in those places. The energy becomes one of love, light, and clarity. It is as though our very souls are freed from captivity.

This experience is similar to the way I feel when I am in the deepest moment of Stillness and am most connected to my loved and loving self. Before we are able to let go of our grudges and our pain, we are tense, clenched, enraged, obsessed, and hurting. We are imprisoned in a cell we have helped to create. We feel disconnected from loved ones, from the flow of life, and, perhaps most important, from ourselves. We may be stuck in our fearful selves, by our own personal choice or by virtue of the fact that we live with fear-filled emotional forces that swirl in our families, institutions, and culture. Regardless of what has trapped us in this position, the addictive powers of fear alter our mood, the speed and texture of our breathing, our brain functioning, and our ability to have perspective on life.

Love as experienced through Forgiveness on the other hand, is a step into being present with one's family, friends, and associates with a clear mind and cleansing breaths. It leaves us connected with our imaginations and our ability to problem solve. It is the gift of oxygen where before there was only shortness of breath, clarity of perception where there were bitter tears.

In each chapter so far we have seen that practicing the Habits of Love can bring us out of our fearful selves into our loving selves, by enhancing the flow of love into our souls and the soul of the larger global family. With the Habit of Forgiveness we come to what is a truly difficult part of the human journey: returning to our free, whole, and open-hearted selves after we have experienced significant pain. Now we address those moments where dishonor, humiliation, injustice, violence, or threats have left us with the central fear that a wrong may not be made right. This injury lodges in us as a kernel of hurt, anger, and resentment that grows exponentially and keeps us trapped in our fearful selves. It is a debilitating way to live and only makes the pain we have suffered live on inside us, continuing to cause us ever more anguish. Many different kinds of experiences can cause this kind of fear to take root in us—from slights and injuries to assaults, abuses, and serious, even heinous, injustices.

No matter the unique catalog of violations each of us has experienced, the underlying issue is whether we will remain stuck in the past or whether we will use the power of Forgiveness to move our own lives forward toward freedom and love. To the degree that we are trapped, we are more likely to lure others into the hurt we are holding inside ourselves—but the Beloved wants us to be a river, not a quagmire.

Becoming Whole

I once was so consumed by an angry offense I was nursing that I thought I could kill. The contempt with which I held a certain person now disgusts me. While the offense was not minor, neither was it catastrophic—and now the transgression itself seems irrelevant. What was devastating at the time was that I was unable to let go of my bitterness. I learned experientially that the Habit of Forgiveness is the only strategy that works to bring an end to an otherwise neverending cycle of score settling. If we are unable to forgive, we are in a vicious cycle in which the score is never actually settled. This is true whether we are seeking to practice Forgiveness at work, in our home, or on a local, national, or global level.

Being stuck in an unforgiving mode wreaks havoc on us. Every minute I thought of this man, my body felt toxic, triggered, and inflamed. After a few weeks, I became aware that most of my day was being consumed by my desire for retaliation. What began to haunt me was that I started disliking the person *I* was turning into. Here I was, giving over a significant amount of my energy to someone who did not warrant that kind of attention. I had given my power away. In addition, I was being increasingly immature in the way I handled other aspects of my life: my marriage, my family, and my work. The resentments I was holding onto were poisoning my life and my relationships.

Then something transformative happened. As I was walking alone, about to cross a traffic intersection in downtown Los Angeles, the man in question drove by. In that instant, I woke up to what I had become: someone boiling in a brew of self-pity and anger. In the same instant, a powerful thought came to me: "I want to be free of being consumed by the thoughts of this person, and the only way to be free is to forgive."

Later that night, when I had a moment of Stillness to think about what had taken place earlier, I understood that I was ready to put my antipathy aside. I genuinely wanted to live a life free of the toxic preoccupation with how I had been wronged. The various Habits of Love that were constantly at play in different aspects of my life were intersecting now, guiding me toward an answer to my problem. These habits—especially of Generosity, Compassion (which we delve into next), and also Play—helped me realize that I wanted to live on the other side of Forgiveness. I was able to form a new perspective that was healing and fruitful. An energy flowed through my body so mightily that it cleansed me of the hatred, fury, and vengeful fantasies that had consumed me. I was literally emancipated, and in becoming free and unburdened I also became whole again.

Just as my own experience stemmed from a somewhat inconsequential incident, many of us who experience injustice or hurt at someone else's hands find it impossible to see our situation in a life-giving perspective. The wrong that has been done to us assumes huge proportions in our memories and imaginations. At the extreme end of the spectrum, we allow that incident to become the defining framework for our entire life. While it is the case that we once were victims, in these instances, we have participated in developing an ongoing victim mentality. Holding a grudge—especially when we continually revisit particularly painful experiences, mentally replaying the infraction over and over again—is an internal signal that we have accepted a victim mentality. But when I contemplate some of the mind-boggling cases I describe in this chapter, my perspective changes and I loosen my own grip on resentment.

Other people have forgiven and continually forgive, and so can we. Every story related here is about the courage of individuals who exercised the Habit of Forgiveness at crucial turning points in their lives. Doing so helped to liberate them from fear, from the prison of not being able to forgive, and from being consumed by a toxic past.

When Life Is Unjust

From an early age we are taught that actions have consequences. As babies, we cry and as a consequence we are fed. As toddlers, when we grab a toy away from another child, we are taught that we must share. In school, we learn that hard work is rewarded with good grades and eager, encouraging teachers. We know that when we eat too much we gain weight, and when we don't take care of our bodies we become less efficient and energetic.

When something happens to upset this balance and counterbalance, it is profoundly disturbing to our sense of order and control. Perhaps life deals us an unjust blow or someone behaves toward us in an unwarranted manner. In the case of Melanie and Jake, parents of three young girls, when they were faced with heartbreaking circumstances that did not seem justified, they dealt with it in dramatically different ways. In one case, it led to eventual healing, and in the other, to a deep depression.

This young family lives in Southern California and embraces an active, outdoor-oriented lifestyle. Both parents are fit and health conscious, and their girls are happy-go-lucky children with many friends and a life filled with soccer, dance, and family dinners. They work hard to ensure their children are safe and happy. About two years ago, the middle daughter, Jayda, thought she had hurt herself playing soccer and began limping. She sat out a few games, but the pain in her knee did not lessen. They took her to a doctor and after weeks of tests it was discovered that Jayda had osteosarcoma, cancer in her bones. She was nine years old.

While Jayda was in treatment, the parents dealt with the calamity fairly well. They were driven by the need to provide emotional encouragement and support for Jayda and the two other girls, and their lives revolved around visits to the oncologist, chemotherapy, and recovery. Jayda, a sturdy, athletic girl with red-blond hair and freckles, was an upbeat child who made friends easily. Everyone in the neighborhood pitched in to help, cooking meals and taking over carpools. The generosity of the community, the flexibility of their employers, and the dedicated care of the doctors and nurses went a long way toward making the ordeal manageable for both Melanie and Jake. And yet, tragically, cancer claimed their daughter's life after a year of heroic struggle.

"We were totally devastated," Jake said. "But after she passed, everything changed—and it felt like we were suddenly all alone in our grief. It was soul destroying." The couple had many friends nearby, but their families live on the East Coast. They began to feel increasingly isolated and depressed. After about six months, their relationship become so strained they started seeing a family therapist. In those sessions it became clear that they were dealing not only with grief at losing their child, but anger at the injustice of it.

"We did everything right, and yet she was still taken from us. I couldn't figure out the rhyme or reason. I was just so furious," Jake explained. "It was as though my heart iced over. I was bitter. I just really needed someone to blame, and there wasn't anyone."

Seeking to find order and reason in our lives when we have experiences that are random and unjust can lead us to harbor bitterness that hinders our ability to make loving choices. While neither Melanie nor Jake could reconcile their daughter's death, Melanie was better able to accept the reality and move forward. The love for her other two children could shine through. Jake, on the other hand, became profoundly depressed. He wanted someone to pay. "I felt the rage of someone trying to point the finger of blame and not knowing where to turn. I was angry at neighbors for living normal lives, friends for laughing and pretending she'd never existed," he said. "There was no one to forgive and yet I desperately needed to forgive someone."

We yearn for life to make sense, for there to be appropriate checks and balances, but this is sadly not always the case. Jake slowly began to take back his own life again when he decided to volunteer once a week in the pediatric cancer ward and continue therapy on his own. Eventually, he was able to be free of his desire for vengeance by healing himself from the inside. Though it was hard won, hope was reborn.

It's Really about *Us*

Melanie and Jake's struggle to reconcile reality with their expectations of a just world shows how the Habit of Forgiveness is much more about the person who is suffering than about the person, event, or circumstance that has caused the pain. Often we struggle with the notion of Forgiveness because of a belief that the offender is the root of the problem. How can we forgive, for example, a hit-and-run driver or an abusive spouse or a negligent surgeon? The gift of the Habit of Forgiveness is that it reverses our tendency to allow the sins of the offender to eclipse the freedom and power of the wounded. In the end, Forgiveness is less about the offender than it is about healing and liberating those who have been hurt. Focusing with so much passion on the person who is in the wrong becomes an excuse to not move forward.

This is a doomed endeavor. We do not have the power over others to teach them a lesson or to control their behavior. Everyone has his or her own journey. Your life may be an inspiration to my life, but your choices cannot control my choices. No one can force another to change by withdrawal or withholding. When we hold a grudge, we are desperate for the person who has wronged us to recognize his or her mistake and change. We seek order and reason, but most often this is futile. In putting all our energies into the desire to change someone else, we deprive ourselves of much-needed energy for our own transformation and growth. We thwart ourselves, putting up roadblocks inside our loving selves.

Connie Domino, one of my guests when I was hosting the *Oprah's Soul Series* radio show and the author of *The Law of Forgiveness*, first introduced me to this idea. Domino describes Forgiveness as a process that is primarily in the service of freeing the person who is doing the forgiving. A critical part of her thesis is that you do not have to reconnect with the wrongdoer in order to forgive, and that freeing yourself through Forgiveness will help you achieve your heart's deepest desires.

I must admit that when I first heard her speak, I was not entirely sold. Many of us find it almost impossible to let go of old hurts. We wonder, "Is everyone really worth forgiving?" You, too, may be thinking of incidents and people you have yet to forgive. Memories of physical violations like sexual abuse, rape, or other instances of sexual misconduct may come to mind when considering what is unforgivable. Harm to our psyche will also beckon: marital infidelity and other personal betrayals, or moments of being publically shamed or criticized. Perhaps workplace politics caused loss of employment, or we were unfairly characterized in print or in gossip. We may have endured thousands of micro-aggressions, tiny paper cuts to the soul, slights and snubs, moments when we were dishonored and excluded.

And yet, when we begin with the desire to become whole by operating from our loving selves as opposed to our fearful selves, we may find that we have actually been our own biggest impediments to Forgiveness. The wonderful corollary to this is that *we* are the only thing that we have any real control over. Leo, a troubled young man I have known for many years, discovered this for himself when he had his first child.

As a boy, Leo had been beaten and berated constantly by a domineering father who was a big drinker. His father left the family when Leo was five. A few years later, he went on to change the course of his life by entering Alcoholics Anonymous. When Leo was 15, his father remarried and had two new children, both boys. Leo felt abandoned. He was angry at his father for the abuse but also deeply disappointed that his father never tried to make amends with him. "He lavished all this love on Josh and Jonah," Leo said, "and forgot all about me." Leo carried this anger inside him for years.

But something changed when Leo started his own family. "I was playing with my baby, just being silly and laughing," he explained, "and it hit me that I was done with the anger. I wanted to forgive my father." At this point, his father had been dead for five years already, and even if he were alive Leo was not certain he would have wanted a reconciliation. But what he came to understand in that moment was that forgiving his father had much less to do with his father than with himself. When he was able to put the past behind him once and for all, he felt truly free in a way he had never really experienced before.

"Forgiveness is really nothing more than an act of self-healing and self-empowerment," said Holocaust survivor Eva Kor. Dr. Josef Mengele experimented on Kor and her twin in the extermination camps at Auschwitz (her parents and sisters were killed), and she forgave him. Later, Kor founded CANDLES Holocaust museum and education center in Indiana in order to promote Forgiveness. "I call it a miracle medicine. It is free, it works and has no side effects."

Free to Move On

Consider athletics in light of the dynamic of Forgiveness: games can be very intense, and sometimes players get carried away by their desire to win. It becomes very personal. One opponent focuses on another player, convinced that he or she is playing unfairly. All the attention turns to "getting back at" that player—putting him in his place, or teaching her a lesson. This can lead to distracted play and infractions; the goal of winning is overshadowed by the desire to get even. One of the most important lessons athletes learn is that to be successful, it is much more effective to focus on their own performance, allowing small grievances to slide, than to worry about settling scores.

This kind of dynamic plays itself out daily in the business world, where we are constantly challenged whether to look forward or backward. John is a friend who recently left his job at a small consulting firm to break out on his own. In the year since he's been his own boss, a few clients have failed to pay him on time, and on one occasion a client did not pay him at all, even though John had completed all the work. Amazingly, these experiences seem to slide off him like water off a duck's back.

How does John manage not to be sidetracked into fear and doubt when faced with such financial insecurity? He remembers advice his father, an architect, gave him when he was a boy. His dad often did design work for friends and family, once designing a beautiful shingled cottage on Cape Cod for a friend he knew from the neighborhood. That friend never paid his bill.

"My mom was just livid, she couldn't get over it," John explained, "but Dad was pretty circumspect about it. He always told me it's better to look ahead and think about the next client, the next opportunity, rather than get stuck in the past, fuming about something that went wrong."

There are certain fundamental assumptions we make as human beings when we engage in a relationship with someone, whether personal or professional. When we have a close friend, we assume he or she will not do anything to hurt us. In a family, we expect to be loved and protected by our parents. In a marriage, we promise to remain true to each other and hold each other's best interests at heart. In more intimate relationships when those expectations are dashed and someone lets us down by his or her behavior, that disloyalty can be especially hard to forgive.

Spouses who stray outside the marriage hurt us in our deepest core because we have allowed ourselves to be vulnerable. In putting their needs or desires ahead of our own, an unfaithful spouse is devaluing our sacrifices, efforts, and needs. But forgiving an adulterous partner does not mean condoning his or her behavior or accepting blame for the circumstances that lead to the betrayal. It means finding a way to move on from the pain.

I am friends with two couples who experienced the trauma of

infidelity and handled it in very different ways: in one case there was reconciliation, and in the other, divorce. But in both cases the injured party chose to move forward in a loving way. In the first instance, that meant reconnecting with the spouse and working on strengthening the relationship and rebuilding the trust. In the other, it meant forging a path alone but with no lingering bitterness toward the former spouse. The ability to forgive offered both parties the chance to heal and face the future with renewed hope and an unburdened spirit.

It is also important to note that a successful marriage requires such a deep and continuous intertwining of lives that even when there is no breach of trust or egregious infraction, everyday irritations can pile up dangerously. We have to forgive the small things so we can move on in life. Whether the occasion for Forgiveness is a minor or a major one, whether it is between intimates, acquaintances, or colleagues, the most important aspect of engaging the Habit of Forgiveness is giving *ourselves* the freedom to move forward in life, looking toward the light ahead of us rather than backward at the dark tunnel of the past.

Desire Alone Sets Us Free

But how do we do it? Sometimes Forgiveness can be immensely difficult, and we may at times despair of being "holy" or "saintly" enough to pull off such a feat. When Jesus said, "Father, forgive them, for they do not know what they are doing" (Luke 23:34 NRSV), he offered no conditions on this Forgiveness. Many people note, quite appropriately, how difficult unqualified Forgiveness is. I agree. In fact, we simply cannot will Forgiveness to take place. But this does not leave us entirely powerless: where we cannot *will* Forgiveness, we can *desire* it.

One Sunday after I delivered my sermon at All Saints, a worshipper named Chris approached me as I was leaving the church. As he grasped my arm and asked whether I had a moment to hear a story, Chris's narrow face broke into a toothy smile. "See, I have to thank you," he said. "I had a huge breakthrough!"

He explained that he had a close friend named Dale who lived on his block when he was a boy. As children they were inseparable, and they stayed in close touch even when they went away to college in different states. When Chris was in his late twenties, he discovered that his high school sweetheart and Dale had had a secret dalliance one summer when Chris was away. This was like a knife to his heart. While he was upset with his former girlfriend, he was furious with Dale. This was an unexpected and painful betrayal of their friendship, and it colored every memory Chris had of his old friend. For almost a decade he nurtured the pain inside him. Though he did not care to forgive Dale, it bothered him greatly that his thoughts so often turned to Dale. He was haunted by a relentless feeling of anger.

A few weeks earlier, Chris had been in church when I gave a sermon on Forgiveness, during which I mentioned that although we often simply cannot bring ourselves to forgive, we can at least desire to forgive. I talked about how the very desire has sufficient power to lead us toward Forgiveness. Chris came to the altar rail to receive communion that morning, and as he knelt he prayed, "I don't even want to forgive, but I do want a desire to forgive. I just wish I could *want to* forgive."

That night, Chris had a vivid dream that he and Dale were children playing games together. They were in the backyard, running around in the sunshine and throwing a football around. When he awoke the next morning, a feeling of happiness and joy infused him. He remembered the laughter and warmth from his dream. As he got dressed, he realized that the feeling of holding a grudge that had gnawed at him for so long had vanished. He felt that he had forgiven his friend. He felt free. And then he said to me that for the very first time in years he sensed that a "higher power" was real and present in his life.

Sometimes we cannot fully forgive someone who has hurt us or someone we love. In those instances it is enough to make the decision that Forgiveness is desirable—that although it may not be possible, it is preferable. My experience is that the empowering energy of the Beloved will meet your desire to forgive, and you will be launched on your journey toward healing.

Walking in Someone Else's Shoes

The core principle of the Habits of Love is that while not everyone behaves lovingly or honorably, everyone is Beloved. The Beloved dwells inside every human being, and the Beloved connects us all in a network of interdependency. What helps in the process of Forgiveness is coming to realize that so much harm comes from those who have not been loved and have not been told that they are loved.

A few years ago, a teacher named Richard was accused of rape by a 15-year-old student of his. Richard is the father of two young children and is a high school basketball coach in his small town in southern Texas. He is well liked and active in his hometown, volunteering with the fire department and often going out of his way to mentor teenagers. The charges against him sent a shock wave rippling through his community and set off a series of events that were devastating to his family. The police visited Richard's home and handcuffed him in front of his children. The family spent hundreds of thousands of dollars hiring a lawyer to defend him against the charges. The community was deeply divided about whether to let Richard continue coaching, and eventually he decided to quit while he awaited trial.

Richard's wife, Hayley, was blindsided. She believed fully in her husband's innocence, and she would eventually be proven right. Initially, her focus was on helping him navigate the legal difficulties and shielding their children from the rumors and terrible anxiety. But soon her focus shifted to the accuser.

"I couldn't understand why she would do this to us," Hayley said. "I knew she had had a tough childhood, but we all have problems. I felt so much rage against her for putting my family through this misery. I wanted to find a reason *why*—why would she try to destroy us when we had never done anything to her?"

The charges were eventually dropped when it was discovered that the girl had made a similar accusation that turned out to be false against the foster family she had lived with previously, in New Mexico. But the anger over her actions and their consequences lingered.

A few years later, Hayley's older daughter cornered her in the kitchen while she was making dinner and asked her about the incident. They had never talked about what happened as a family. In reopening all the old wounds, Hayley realized she had not yet moved past the bitterness at the emotional—and financial—wounds this girl had inflicted on them, even though she hadn't seemed to be aware of the ramifications of her accusations when she made them. A minister from Hayley's church suggested she visualize the girl as a baby, then a toddler, then a young adult.

"I imagined cradling her in my arms, and looking at her as I had looked at my own children when they were born," she said. "But instead of feeling love, I began weeping. What I realized was that she had never felt that love. No one had ever given her the attention she deserved. She went from being evil in my mind to being human." While it didn't make the wrongs right and it didn't excuse her lies, it did help Hayley release the debilitating anger she had not been able to let go.

Forgiving Ourselves

The Habit of Forgiveness can also mean we must forgive ourselves for behavior we feel we may have deserved. Forgiveness of self may be the hardest and deepest place that Forgiveness must reach. We often hear of cases in which people who have been abused believe they are somehow responsible because they angled for attention or drew the ire of the abuser. For instance, children who have been assaulted by family members sometimes suffer in silence for years because they believe themselves to have been the cause of the problem. My dear friend Janet is a prime example of someone who has moved beyond the pain inflicted on her by engaging in self-forgiveness. The details of the tragic abuse she suffered at the hands of her father are her story to tell, but they led her into a disastrous marriage, an alcohol addiction, and numerous devastating medical complications.

In searching for a way to make sense of the pain inflicted on her, it was easier for Janet to blame herself rather than her husband or father. This is twisted logic to be sure. When that happens, however, the first step toward healing requires those who have been hurt to recognize that they are not responsible for someone else's behavior. The second step is to remember they are truly loved and to forgive themselves for whatever they think may have contributed to allowing the abuse to happen or continue.

"I think the key to forgiveness is to know oneself as deeply loved and deeply forgiven," Janet once told me. "If there's someone who I need to forgive, then I also need to be forgiven for the resentment against that person that I've been carrying around. Without this self-forgiveness, I think forgiveness is a mere mental concept."

It is so much easier to forgive other people when we no longer believe we have to be perfect either. By releasing fantasies of our own perfection, self-forgiveness makes it possible for us to forgive others, thereby freeing the resentments and hatred we have carried inside us. Through self-forgiveness we release the part of the perpetrator that we may have internalized and identified as part of ourselves, and that in turn alleviates the burden of carrying that negative energy. I think of an incident I heard of in which a father ferociously beat his daughter with a belt after she disobeyed him. The mother, trapped for years in this violent relationship, tried to intervene by taking the belt away, hitting the daughter herself, and then leaving the room. Though she was attempting to put an end to the whipping, she actually contributed to it—first by allowing it to continue unreported, and second by partaking in it herself.

The mother eventually separated from the father and filed for divorce. Later, she berated herself for her weakness in permitting a culture of fear and violence to dominate her family for so long. Had she been more courageous, she thought, she could have saved her daughter from the trauma of this oppression. In taking steps to protect herself and her child, she first had to give up the defeatism and vulnerability that self-blame can inflict. She needed to free herself from the mentality of being a victim. Once she established herself on more solid ground, she was able to forgive herself for her failings as a mother and thereby move on with her life—toward becoming a better mother.

Being a parent is surely one of the greatest challenges we face as individuals. It is all too common to worry compulsively that we are not doing a good enough job, believing that our all-too-human failings will negatively impact our children. But in understanding that we are not perfect and should not hold ourselves to impossible standards, we free ourselves to focus on what we are good at. We each have strengths and we each have weaknesses. Forgiving ourselves for those areas of weakness lets us put our energy into those areas where we might excel.

The journey through Forgiveness may be more or less extreme for us, and yet no matter the level of the infraction that raises the need for Forgiveness, the underlying issue at stake is constant. It is our ability to have love coursing through our veins instead of yielding to the grudge holding and revenge fantasies of fear. What hangs in the balance is whether we believe, first, that we can be healed. If we do, then Forgiveness, even in the face of dramatic torture and murder, can be accomplished.

The Habits of Love ask us to take responsibility for our state of being; that's where maturity lies. As we observed, the individual we seek to forgive does not have to change in order for us to free ourselves. And we do not have to let down our barriers of self-protection or the legal boundaries and protections that a just society provides. We only have to dismantle the barrier inside us—the barrier that stops our loving selves from being free.

Playing the Blame Game

There are, however, people who carve out a niche for themselves as the ones who will never forgive, regardless of the circumstance. They have created their identity around their victimhood, no matter how far away from their true selves this false identity is. These are the "injustice collectors." Playing the victim is the only script they know, and in always seeing themselves in that role they give up their ability to move on with their lives. I know a young man who can remember every wrong he endured as a child, and he carries those feelings with him into his personal relationships and even his work. Instead of seeing himself as the one with the power to make choices, he assumes that every other person will step onto the stage of his life playing the role of persecutor. Were he able to free himself of this mentality and embrace Forgiveness, he would find empowerment in all the other areas of his life that currently pose such a challenge for him.

My mentor, Rabbi Friedman, taught me that one of the largest impediments to any family healing from dysfunction is when the entire family accommodates itself to one member who insists on playing the role of "injustice collector." These individuals are so absorbed by all the minor misfortunes and occasional calamities that have occurred that they endlessly rehearse the litany of what they have suffered. Even a conversation about current events becomes an association with the catalog of ways people do appalling things. They have made the mistake of thinking that their misfortunes define them, and that misfortune is the way the world works. These individuals exist not only in families, of course, but also in businesses, groups of colleagues or friends, or any other collection of persons. But they often flourish especially virulently in a family, where others feel obligated to support such a world-view due to the bonds of blood—or else suffer ostracism, where the injustice collector demonizes those who are trying to break free.

Such was the case with a parishioner of mine, Jerome. After years of a broken marriage, he and his wife separated. At the time of separation, Jerome was badly wounded, spiritually and emotionally. So hurt, in fact, that on the day that he moved out of the family home, he began to lose his voice. In retrospect, this was symbolic of the strain in his life at that point. In the midst of such brokenness he was forced to question many things about himself: Was he capable or deserving of love? Where was God in all of this? How could he be a good father to his son when he was so damaged?

The energy of the Beloved coming through many in his community helped him answer these questions and to weather the storm of a bitter divorce that took three and a half years to complete. Facing the mother of his child during their first court appearance, Jerome had to listen to outright lies. In addition, she reeled off every way that he had ever erred in word or deed. The attacks were vicious and continuous, distorting facts and omitting key mitigating circumstances. She failed to take any responsibility for what had befallen their marriage. His wife would deliberately tell their son things to upset him and turn him against his father. She even went so far as to allege that their son had serious learning disabilities when she thought it might help her custody case.

These are wounding actions, especially from someone we have loved and hoped to build a life with. When hope has been shattered, it can be particularly hard to forgive. Jerome shared some of these details with his ministers, one of whom insisted that he needed to forgive his now ex-wife. Jerome did not believe it was possible, but the minister did not give up.

"At first my attempts were mechanical; I just couldn't truly forgive her in my heart," Jerome said. "But as I continued to practice forgiveness, I realized that the pain, heaviness, and anxiety that I experienced in her presence and when thinking about the divorce were just as much about my unwillingness to forgive and not let go as they were about my ex's actions."

When he recognized that her behavior was coming from a place of fear, he began to feel the strength he needed to deal with her continuing bad conduct. Even with the divorce finalized, she continues to raise hell from time to time. "In those moments I realize that I have a choice to make. It's not always easy, that's for sure, and I can't say that I always immediately go to a place of love and forgiveness. But by having forgiven in the past, it's like riding a bike." This has enabled him to spend the time he has with his son free of regret and anger toward his former wife. She no longer dominates his every thought, and he is more able to find enjoyment in everyday activities again.

People like Jerome's wife are present in our lives in many forms. They can be part of our immediate families. They can be co-workers or old friends. These individuals establish fear as the primary mode of operation. In dealing with them, we often slip into a place of fear as well. Schemes of retaliation and instant replays of "the crime" flood our imaginations, and we assume a new identity, cultivating a persona of self-pity until we are no longer connected and available to our partner, children, friends, and most of all to our loving selves. We become a victim and we give up our power. But embracing love and opening our hearts saves us from this trap.

When Forgiveness Heals Others

Though the Habit of Forgiveness is largely about regulating ourselves instead of trying to regulate others, it can on occasion profoundly affect someone who has done wrong, even the perpetrator
of a crime. On September 11, 2001, a young man sitting in his
apartment in Dallas was watching the attacks on the Twin Towers
at the World Trade Center in New York as they unfolded on television. Mark Stroman imagined that his sister was at work on a top
floor of the North Tower. Feeling personally under siege, and that
his right to live in peace and security had been shattered, he went
on a drug-fueled, deadly rampage for several days. He was desperate
for someone else to share his pain.

Carrying a shotgun, he entered three Dallas area convenience
stores and gas stations hunting down "Arabs," who symbolized for
him those who had attacked the United States. At each store he
shot a clerk. Two of the men died: Waqar Hasan was Pakistani,
and Vasudev Patel was from India. The third man, Rais Bhuiyan, a
Bangladeshi Muslim, survived. Years after being arrested, convicted,
and sentenced to death, Stroman was still bragging that he was an
"Arab slayer."

Gunshot wounds left Bhuiyan blind in his right eye. Three dozen
shotgun pellets are still embedded in his face. But Bhuiyan says
his Muslim faith teaches Forgiveness, and that Forgiveness brings
"peace and healing in our society, in our country." In a stunning
show of the healing power of Forgiveness, he worked tirelessly to
prevent Stroman's execution, which took place on July 20, 2011.
Working with attorneys through the eleventh hour, Bhuiyan said,
"I believe if Mark is given a chance to live, he will become a
spokesperson in raising awareness for hate crimes. If he can educate
one person who is full of hate, that is an achievement."

The energy of love, delivered through the Habit of Forgiveness,
opened the doors of the perpetrator's loving self. As Stroman faced
his execution, he was a changed man. "I've come from a person

with hate embedded into him into a person with a lot of love and understanding for all races...I received a message that Rais loved me and that is powerful," said Stroman, who suffered extreme abuse and neglect as a child at the hands of his alcoholic parents, according to court records.

We can't always count on perpetrators' confessions or expressions of remorse, or trust that they will turn around their lives. Waiting for wrongdoers to change before we forgive them places too many conditions on our own freedom. What if the person is dead? Would we simply say to ourselves, "Sorry, you are doomed to the ball and chain of this past horror forever?"

Love calls us to be available to people in the present who need our vigor and abilities. Practicing the Habit of Forgiveness allows us to embrace our loving selves at a time when our fearful selves may appear all but unconquerable.

How to Practice Forgiveness

Practicing the Habit of Forgiveness requires a receptive or amenable mind-set—an openness to going on an adventure beyond our hurts and beyond the fears our milieu has instilled in us. The absence of Forgiveness in one's life actually blocks living a bold and brave life grounded in the knowledge that we are all different and have important creative gifts to offer the world. Refusing self-forgiveness limits our ability to make those imaginative contributions to life that no one else can. It is in that spirit that we even consider forgiving others.

As with some of the other Habits of Love, achieving Forgiveness takes much practice over time. Life offers us unending opportunities to forgive. We cannot force ourselves to forgive, and trying to do so particularly when we are being insincere does not work. If we are caught in the constant trap of seeing things only from yesterday's personal perspective, we are allowing ourselves to remain in the victim role instead of breaking free. Rather than insisting on others changing or making amends, we must focus on the responsibilities that are in our court.

The Habit of Forgiveness asks us to engage all the other Habits of Love on our journey toward discovering how Forgiveness can flow through us. Forgiveness unlocks the prison of fear, self-punishment, and revenge and sends us into the world rehabilitated for a fresh future.

Every habit in this book asks us on which terms we are living in this world: those of fear or those of love? In learning to practice Forgiveness, we answer resoundingly that we are choosing to live according to the Habits of Love with an open heart and an open mind.

* Coming to Stillness is a prerequisite for Forgiveness. You don't have to attain the serenity we imagine residing in the center of the Buddha or Jesus. It is enough to become aware of the harmful effects on your life of not forgiving. It is enough to sit quietly until names or faces or events surface that need your Forgiveness. Give yourself enough time that you do not feel rushed. As you think about past grievances, you may begin to feel uncomfortable physical sensations, such as a hot face, a bitter lump in your throat, or clenched muscles. Accept that this process can be difficult and persevere.

* You may be surprised at the grievances you are still holding, or you may be seized by an immediate situation in your personal life. If several occasions for Forgiveness arise, it may help to make a list, and keep that list in a safe place like a journal while you work through Forgiveness. Your goal will be to make this list unnecessary.

* Choose a person on your list and imagine him or her in your mind's eye. Imagine him or her bathed in the healing light of the Beloved. Imagine that person as his or her loving self, not as the mean, egocentric or fearful self that harmed you. You will most certainly encounter mental and perhaps even physical resistance to this process. There is

anger or fear or pain in your heart blocking the ability of your loving energy to flow through you. This is to be expected. Keep trying to imagine the person or people you are thinking of standing in a warm and nurturing light. Imagine yourself in that same healing light.

Make an affirmation of Forgiveness that you can repeat to yourself. Consider Connie Domino's affirmation, which several people in this chapter and thousands of others have used. In it she states, "I forgive you completely and freely, I release you and let you go. So far as I'm concerned, the incident that happened between us is finished forever. I wish the best for you. I wish for you your highest good. I hold you in the light. I am free and you are free, and all again is well between us. Peace be with you." (Domino recommends using the same affirmation in forgiving yourself and for others to forgive you.) If these exact words don't work for you, try using others. The key is to try to let go of your resentment and wish the best for offenders, rather than wishing them ill.

Remember that you are not committing to building a new relationship with this person or persons. You do not have to become friends again, or even interact in any way. After I saw the man who had wronged me sitting in his car at that traffic light, I did not ever encounter him again. My goal was not to resume a relationship, but to let go of an old one that was eating away at me. Similarly, you may find that when you take the pressure off by accepting there is no need to rebuild or resume a connection, you will finally be able to take that step toward Forgiveness.

If there are emotional or even legal and physical boundaries you need to secure around yourself to reduce or eliminate the hurt and harm, find someone appropriate who can help you protect yourself. This process is about healing yourself and setting yourself free, and to do so you have the right to feel safe.

As you go through your process, remember that some persons will continue their harmful or hurtful behavior. Frequently that is part of our daily reality. You will simply allow the power of love to assert itself over the power of fear, and from that spiritual place in your core, offer a sincere prayer or wish that the other person may become whole. As we said before, no one can force another to change by withdrawal from a relationship or withholding affection. Understanding this is the beginning of the Habit of Compassion, the habit to which we now turn.

CHAPTER SEVEN

The Habit of Compassion

though sometimes it is necessary
.to reteach a thing its loveliness,
to put a hand on its brow
of the flower
and retell it in words and in touch
it is lovely
until it flowers again from within, of self-blessing

—Galway Kinnell

While Compassion is not the hardest Habit of Love to understand, it can be the most difficult to accept and put into practice. It asks us to act upon the belief that every human being is inherently good, and for many of us this seems an impossible task.

Forgiveness is a natural lead in to the practice of Compassion. In Forgiveness we focus on what has been done to us; in Compassion we focus on what someone may be doing to us *and to others*. When we are able to see beyond a person's harmful behavior and find the goodness lurking deep in the shadows, our recognition helps bring that goodness to light, sparking the reawakening of that person's loving self. In the exercise of the Habit of Compassion we are giving someone else a gift.

A young teacher from Boston was challenged by this distinction herself two years ago. Running along the Charles River one evening as dusk was beginning to fall, Jennifer was assaulted by a group of young men. This packed-earth pathway that wound its way along the magnificent river had been her sanctuary since she was a child, and Jennifer often went there for walks or runs to contemplate life and make important decisions. After the attack, it was no longer a place of Stillness for her, but a place of fear. She tried to conquer the fear and reclaim this place for herself by walking there with friends, but instead of feeling less anxious, Jennifer felt more so. She was often sweating and shaking, unable to move past her fear.

Nighttime became an endless exercise in staring blankly at her alarm clock, wishing for sleep to return. At school during the day, she was often lackluster and tired. Jennifer had been known for her easy smiles and boundless energy, and people began to notice her change of demeanor. She visited a therapist, who helped her explore the idea that the young men who had hurt her were themselves wounded. She eventually found Forgiveness in her heart. While this helped ease her pain, it did not entirely release her from her fear. There were days when it was an effort to break a smile for her students. She stopped calling her friends and going out socially.

Stuck in a defensive mode, she could not find a way to reengage with her loved and loving self. Gathering all her courage, she called a drug treatment center in the city to ask about running a writing workshop there. They referred her to a halfway house for young offenders in Hyde Park. This was a home for older teens who were trying to find their way back into a regular life. Jennifer arranged to teach there once a week on Thursdays, after her classes ended for the day.

At first, entering the dilapidated house with the dented plastic siding, she battled severe nerves. Facing the group, a mental health aide by her side, she asked them each to tell their story. Eventually, they wrote their stories up, worked with Jennifer on editing them, and then held a reading to which they invited family members.

These damaged souls had stories to tell, and in helping them release their own pain, Jennifer released hers too. It was easier for her to smile and find joy in the everyday. She emerged from her cocoon and began meeting friends downtown in the evenings again. And in rediscovering the Beloved within herself, she helped these men rediscover the Beloved dwelling deep within themselves too.

Like Jennifer, when we practice the Habit of Compassion we are making a choice to reflect for others something they no longer can see in themselves. While this enhances our own sense of goodness, it is, most important, an extraordinary gift of love to give another.

The Beloved Resides in Us All

One evening, the author and religious scholar Andrew Harvey was strolling on the beach in a seaside town in his native India, immersed in thought. All of a sudden he saw a divine light radiating upward from the footprints he had left behind on the warm beach sand. He felt awed and proud to be singled out in this way—and then, as he looked around him, he was taken aback: at the very same time that divine light was radiating from his own footprints, that same light was radiating from everybody else's footprints too.

As Harvey experienced, we all have within us the divine light of the Beloved; each of us—no matter how conventional, extraordinary, or errant we may seem—is more than a sum of what we have done in our lives. It is natural to fear that goodness has been obliterated in some people, but the Habit of Compassion releases us from this fear. We come to trust that certain persons who seem to be without conscience and soul can once again be an instrument of goodness. This Habit of Compassion is deeper than any religion, although most world religions in their original forms were founded on it.

The theological reasoning behind the belief in the goodness of every human being is pretty simple. In the beginning was the power of love. Each of us was made by and through that power. Because love—the Beloved, which is within all of us and constitutes our loving self—made every human being, each of us has the power of that Belovedness at our core. We may not think of it this way consciously, especially those of us who are not versed in traditional religious thinking. Religions often refer to this Beloved core as *the image of God*. I think of it as simply the loving spirit that dwells inside each of us, to which every human being can have access through the Habits of Love.

When any of us aligns our behavior or identifies ourselves with a fear-based storyline or script, we lose touch with our open-hearted selves, and our fearful selves emerge. But when a person or an event helps us remember who we really are as human beings, reminding us of the potential for goodness that we all have within us, we experience the power of Compassion. When we exercise the Habit of Compassion toward another person, we contribute to the possibility of goodness flowering in that person again.

It is easy enough to feel Compassion for some people: an innocent like Jennifer, for example, or a child who has been abused. But the Habit of Compassion asks us to extend that same consideration and benevolence to the persons who committed the crime against the innocent. The boys who hurt Jennifer, the man who damaged his child, the thief who pilfered money from his company.

This does not mean we condone heinous behavior or underplay the seriousness of these transgressions. In a just society, there must still be accountability within the rule of law. What it does mean, though, is that we understand that the perpetrators are also in pain, and that we believe there is goodness and light at their core. All is not lost. By extending our Compassion in such difficult cases we are helping that person find, once again, his or her own loved and loving self. We are affirming the potential for healing.

Finding the Spark of Holiness

One spring, Archbishop Desmond Tutu came to preach at All
Saints. His theme that day was that all human beings are "God
carriers," with no exceptions. Sitting in the wooden pews among
the other esteemed guests that morning was Rabbi Joshua Levine-
Grater. He had been quite nervous about attending the service:
Archbishop Tutu's strong criticisms of the Israeli occupation of
Palestine have made him unwelcome in many parts of the Jewish
community. The rabbi knew that many of his own congregants
would rather he picket Tutu's sermon than attend and learn from it.
The rabbi chose the latter.

That day he was deeply moved by the archbishop's assertion that
every person on earth is a piece of God who therefore is holy and
deserves respect, dignity, compassion, and love. I think the rabbi
would have been grateful for that insight alone—but Tutu pushed
his thinking even further.

After hearing the sermon at my church, Rabbi Levine-Grater began thinking more than ever about the differences between living
ethically and living holy—between setting up a society that seeks
justice and equality for all, and a society that goes even further and
actively seeks the holy in other people. As the rabbi later said, "It is
easy to love those similar to you, to love those you already love. To
be holy, to be God carriers, is to love those you don't like, even those
you hate—to find the spark of holiness, the spark of God, in every
person, in every human being."

Once a week, the rabbi holds a meditation group in his syna-
gogue. On the Tuesday after Tutu's sermon, a group of congregants
came together to talk quietly, and to sit in Stillness and meditate.
The rabbi thought of the words of the great Hassidic masters, particularly Ba'al Shem Tov and Rebbe Nachman of Breslov, who called
upon us to love our enemies, to pray for those whom we despise,
and most powerfully, "when we see evil in others, use it as a mirror
to see what is wrong with ourselves."

He shared these thoughts with those gathered. An elderly woman in attendance, wearing the faint blue tattoo on her forearm of a Holocaust survivor, turned to the rabbi, took a deep breath, and then looked around at the others. "In my darkest days in the concentration camps," she said, "when I was losing hope, I thought to myself, *There must be some humanity in Hitler, perhaps when he is listening to music, the music he loved so much, maybe at that moment, for a split second, he is human.* And that gave me hope to try and keep living."

Everyone in the room was shocked into silence. As the rabbi said in his own sermon to his congregation three nights later, "Who could say that other than a survivor and not be vilified, not be seen as sick and twisted?"

The corollary to a belief that all human beings are essentially good is that destructive behaviors that we characterize as inhumane or even as inhuman are expressions of a wrongdoer's pain or illness. This can be hard to swallow—and is often why it is easier to engage Forgiveness within ourselves first, before being able to contemplate true Compassion for others. Yet once we release from ourselves the deep barbs of hurt that abuse can inflict, it becomes progressively easier to see an adversary as human at the level of *being*. Somewhere along their journey, our adversaries were taught to hate and to live from their fearful selves, unaware of or forgetting that their loving selves are bound to all others. Those who live from their loving selves resist those expressions of hatred, injustice, and violence toward others and themselves. At the same time, they see in the perpetrators of hatred, injustice, and violence, a loveliness and goodness that remains unaccessed.

Unconditional Love

Thomas Merton argued that the Hebrew word *hesed*, which is often translated as *compassion*, is a picture word. He suggested we visualize a healthy parent cradling a baby. When that parent looks into the baby's eyes, he or she cannot help but love that child. The seventeenth-century Italian Baroque painting *Saint Joseph and the Infant Christ*, by Giovanni Battista Gaulli (known as Baciccio), vividly depicts this feeling Merton describes as Compassion by projecting it onto God. In the painting, Joseph, Jesus's father, cradles the infant who is reaching with a pudgy hand for his beard. The delight on Joseph's face as he gazes at this child is stunning. Merton claims this is how the Beloved gazes at each one of us. The Beloved cannot help but find delight in the Belovedness of every human being.

It is a great experience to allow ourselves to feel that kind of love coming toward us from the very power that created the cosmos. And it is a totally liberating and hopeful experience to allow ourselves to feel that kind of love embracing every being in creation. That, I am sure, is what Jesus meant when he said, "The kingdom of God is within you" (Luke 17:21 NKJV). When we allow the energy of Compassion to flow into us and then out to others—particularly those whose behavior is odious to us—we have entered the "kingdom" experience.

Father Gregory Boyle, known as "G" to those he works with, is a Jesuit priest who founded the largest gang-intervention organization in the United States, called Homeboy Industries. Its tagline is "Nothing stops a bullet like a job." While working in the California prison system, Father Greg met a former gang member named Miguel. As a young boy, Miguel had been mistreated, abused, and finally completely abandoned by his family, and he turned to a gang to fill the void his loved ones had left behind. Young Miguel took a violent journey through Los Angeles gang life, was convicted of multiple crimes, and was sent away to prison before he was even twenty years old. After he was released, Father Greg put him to work in the graffiti-removal project of Homeboy Industries.

One New Year's Day, Father Greg's telephone rang. "Happy New Year, G," said a voice in a strong Latino accent. It was Miguel.

"You know, Miguel, it's strange—I was thinkin' of ya on Christmas!" Greg said. He knew that Miguel had no family to welcome him in and had wondered where he was and what he was doing to celebrate. Had Miguel been alone that day?

"Oh no," Miguel answered quickly. "I invited homies from the crew—you know, *vatos* like me who didn't had no place to go for Christmas." He named the five young men who had come over to spend the day with him in his tiny apartment.

Greg was incredulous. He knew each one of those men—they had all been enemies from rival gangs. He asked Miguel what he did on Christmas Day with these former enemies.

"Well," Miguel said, "you're not gonna believe this…but…I cooked a turkey." His voice swelled with pride. He said he had prepared it "ghetto-style."

Greg laughed and told him that he was not really familiar with that recipe.

"You just rub it with a gang a' butter, throw a bunch a' salt and pepper on it, squeeze a couple of *limones* over it, and put it in the oven. It tasted proper."

It must have been quite a scene in that spare apartment in the barrio. As Father Greg writes in his book, *Tattoos on the Heart,* "One would be hard-pressed to imagine something more sacred and ordinary than these six orphans staring at an oven together. It is the entire law and the prophets, all in one moment, right there, in this humble holy kitchen."

Here was a young man who had been orphaned, beaten, abused, and yet had learned to be resilient and magnanimous—the kind of person who gathers enemies together for a meal in his own home. The Compassion extended to him by Father Greg allowed the Beloved in Miguel to blossom once again, as it had when he was still an innocent child, open to receiving the love in the world. Compassion, as practiced by Father Greg and his co-workers, is the act of seeing beneath the surface of behavior, regardless of what level of offense we may feel has been committed.

From the most deeply etched occasions of pain to the relatively trivial, we are constantly being offered a choice of whether or not we will demonize someone who appears as our adversary. It might be the boss at work who is relentlessly backstabbing. The teacher who seems to have it in for us. The parent who cannot stop criticizing and judging us. Or perhaps it is someone who has done us, or our family, unimaginable harm.

Later, working side by side in the Homeboy warehouse, Father Greg turned to Miguel and asked how he did it, given all the pain he had suffered.

Miguel had his answer ready. "You know, I always suspected that there was something of goodness in me, but I just couldn't find it. Until one day."—he quieted a bit—"one day, I discovered it, here, in my heart. I found it…goodness. And ever since that day, I have always known who I was."

He paused and then, looking Father Greg in the eye, said, "And now, nothing can touch me."

When Love Is Withheld

Father Greg speaks about the conditionality of gangs and contrasts it to the unconditional quality of genuine love. "Gangs are bastions of conditional love—one false move, and you find yourself outside. Slights are remembered, errors in judgment held against you forever. If a homie doesn't step up to the plate, perform the required duty, he can be relegated to 'no good' status," he writes. Though it may sound shocking, many religious groups, business institutions, and nations act like gangs; they are bastions of conditional love or even regard.

When family really works, it contains people who have known you at your worst—and whom you have known at their worst. In healthy families, there is a shared understanding that we are all of us better than the worst thing we ever did. Yet in every family there are moments when Compassion seems not to be available. Usually that is because someone of authority in the family is too scared to care. The behavior of one member of the family is simply too threatening to the family system or to the larger cultural system.

A young African American man called in over Skype when I was a guest on the *Oprah Winfrey Show*. He'd been born in the Deep South, in Alabama, and was now living in Atlanta, Georgia. He explained to me that he was struggling with constant overspending. During our conversation, he mentioned in passing that he was gay. This instantly gave me pause: I know the Southern culture quite well, and I could imagine what it might be like to be a gay black man in Alabama and Georgia in the early twenty-first century.

"Do you feel alone?" I asked.

"Yes," he answered, "I do."

My heart went out to him. He seemed lonely, with one of his only connections to Compassion being the *Oprah Winfrey Show* and the online community it so helpfully provides people throughout the world. I said that it was very important for him not to feel isolated and not to isolate himself. I told him that I know many accepting and welcoming people and communities in Atlanta, where he was living. Was he aware of welcoming resources? I asked, and he said that he was. The entire exchange felt embraced by the power of Compassion. One human being connecting to another human being across myriad cultural, racial, and other divides.

As a way of driving home the point that he was a special gift from the Beloved, I said, without any sort of strategy, "Being gay is a gift from God, but our culture doesn't understand that."

Oprah turned to me, astonishment written on her face. "Well, you are the first minister I have ever heard saying being gay is a gift from God, I can tell you that!" The panel, which also included Michael Bernard Beckwith and Elizabeth Lesser, laughed and then began talking earnestly about the meaning behind what I had said. Those words, "Being gay is a gift from God," set up ripples that several years later, after being shared hundreds of thousands of times on YouTube, still impact others.

Not long thereafter, my mother received a telephone call from a friend of hers in our small South Georgia hometown. The caller was crying so hard she could barely talk. She had just watched the show and was thinking of her own son, who had died several years earlier of AIDS.

"Mrs. Bacon, my son was gay," she said to my mother. "I'm crying because he never heard anyone say anything like what your son said on TV today. If he had heard anyone—especially a minister—tell him that being gay was a gift from God, I believe he would be alive today."

As with all of the habits, practicing Compassion benefits from working in increments. You may find it easier to have Compassion for someone who has committed a particular infraction in your life, or even a certain crime, than others, depending on the nature of how your fearful self was formed. We all have different backgrounds and "triggers," different traumatic experiences, whether personal, familial, or cultural. Yet if I have a class of people with whom I don't practice Compassion, I sabotage my own belief in its application to myself. Any time we dehumanize, demonize, or too readily categorize any person, we cut ourselves off from the foundation of our own humanity. This mother was able to move beyond the barrier of her fears and accept the beauty and love that was residing in her deceased son.

Be Free of Fear

Laura is a friend who looks most comfortable in the unadorned, tailored suits associated with her New England family's roots. She has a regal demeanor and tends to be rather restrained until her patience is tested. Francesca is originally from Mexico; she thrives on fiery give-and-take conversations over tables laden with spicy foods and the courtroom where she fights as an attorney for victims of abuse. These two women are among the most brilliant people I have ever known: intelligent, opinionated, strong willed, intrepid and fierce pioneers in peace, justice, inclusion, and human rights issues. Their personalities could not be more different, yet they are effective in their own very different universes.

Ellington was married to Laura and is now married to Francesca, who is pregnant with their first child. Despite a bitter divorce-court battle and wounding behind-the-scenes confrontations and accusations, Laura, Francesca, and Ellington have worked out an admirable joint custody arrangement for his two older children, Susan and Dave. Those kids, now quickly approaching their teens, do not exhibit any extraordinary negative behaviors. Their parents and stepmother have generously put their welfare above all the un-deniable animosity of the divorce and remarriage journey. But the animus and all its accompanying fears remain.

Susan, Ellington and Laura's daughter, was being confirmed, and the entire family was planning to attend a luncheon to celebrate this important rite of passage. The night before, Francesca emailed me in a panic. "This will be the first time father and mother plus all of us sit down together sharing lunch... I have so much trepidation... I got Susan a pretty gift from Mexico City... It is so hard to be truthful about all of these feelings... please give me a few words."

In her plea I heard the fear of where her anger might lead her during what was supposed to be a joyous occasion. In response, I wrote, "Remember that at your core you are nothing but beautiful, beloved goodness. Get in touch with that. And remember that Laura is also nothing but beautiful, beloved goodness. All the horri-ble behavior you have felt from her has been coming from her false and fearful self." I recommended that she take some Stillness into her soul and allow this to guide her treatment of Laura. "Make an internal spiritual bow to Laura's loving self no matter what and you will be free of fear the entire time."

Francesca immediately thanked me and told me that my words brought tears to her eyes.

Those tears did not surprise me. Compassion stirs the deepest parts of our being, and it is often within reach when we consider our own children, or the children of those who are close to us. In 1985, at the height of the Cold War, Sting sang in his song "Russians" that it is through our offspring that we experience our common humanity, as Russians love their children, too. This touches on the very demonization we have been discussing in this chapter.

This feeling of being pervaded by a cosmic Compassion may not have been your experience during your formative years; the faces that gazed upon you may not have had Joseph's beatific acceptance, encouragement, authorization, and sheer joy. My mother often says that family is "better than medicine." She works hard to make sure that is the case in our family. On the other hand, I have seen the inner workings of enough families to know that that is not always the case. Family can be toxin rather than tonic. Perhaps you are a child whose family has turned away from you because of your political orientation or spiritual beliefs, or because you have broken unspoken cultural rules. Or you may be a parent whose grown child cannot treat you with Compassion.

We often need to look for the healing, affirming, and transformative power of Compassion outside our families. The key to Compassionate assistance is finding someone who believes that we have a future that is much brighter than the gloomy predicament in which we currently find ourselves and can transmit that hope deep into our souls. It is the vision that the Compassionate person has about us that makes all the difference. A vision that we can be new, that we can be different, that we can have a fresh start, and that there is something precious, creative, loving, and sacred alive in us. All of these are forms of believing that the Beloved dwells inside us. As Miguel said about discovering goodness inside himself, "Nothing can touch me now."

Compassion Aids Healing

As a young pastor, I encountered the toughest customer in my entire career. Carolyn had enjoyed professional success and was a long-time parishioner, and so sat on several church committees. More often than not, when I expressed my opinion about a matter in one of our meetings, she would turn toward me and roll her eyes. Her posture stiffened and invariably something sarcastic or hurtful would come out of her mouth. It was a constant source of pain for me as I felt myself being attacked and I could not understand why.

This went on for many months, creating a great deal of tension for everyone. Finally, after a meeting was adjourned late one evening, another leader on one of the committees stayed behind to talk to me. "You know," she said with a kind smile, "many of us think that a priest kicked Carolyn's puppy one day when she was a child."

"What do you mean?" I asked.

"Well, you're the third priest we've had at our church that Carolyn treats this way. It's got to stem from her childhood."

The next time I saw Carolyn I asked to speak with her. I had prepared myself to practice the Habit of Candor with her, but I was surprised on that day how far my Candor went when aided by Compassion, when I did not choose to demonize her.

We stood in an alcove of the church, under a small window, where it was quiet. "I have noticed your animosity to me," I said. I recounted the theory that something from her childhood may be going on and then I said, "Carolyn, it is really hard being in a meeting with you when you become sarcastic and angry with me. I don't think this is who you really are. I am trying not to take it personally. But sometimes it gets difficult. I did want you to know that I don't think this is who you really are."

At this point, Carolyn began to weep. We stood in silence, honoring the tears. Then she said, "I need to leave. Please excuse me."

We never approached this delicate matter again. However, from that moment on she seemed to express a more tender side of herself in meetings. I never knew how she had processed our conversation; it was not my business to demand such knowledge. I had expressed Compassion to her by telling her I recognized the Beloved within her. That was my modest contribution to her journey.

These experiences are commonplace in the work world, where we are often thrown together with virtual strangers and yet are called upon to find common ground in stressful situations. We may not understand a colleague's motivation and find it hard to see beyond the surface of their manners, inhibiting our capacity for Compassion. Many years ago, Steve worked in the hotel business in Paris for a year after graduate school. Frequently, the hotel was overbooked and employees had to turn away tired, angry travelers late at night. Six weeks into Steve's stint there, Johannes arrived from a small hotel school in the Black Forest. For the life of him, Johannes could not figure out the hotel's booking system, and Steve constantly had to fix his mistakes. On top of this, Johannes was short tempered and defensive, and seemed both incapable and unwilling to learn the correct steps.

It was clear that before long he would be fired. Late one night, after Steve had helped him yet again, Johannes snapped a nasty retort at him. It would have been easy for Steve to walk away, letting the chips fall where they may. Instead, he turned to his co-worker and asked, "Let's talk, okay?"

After work, they went to a local café in an alley behind the hotel to get a beer. As soon as they sat down, Johannes's shoulders dropped and his face softened. He confessed that being in the "big leagues" in a large international hotel made him so nervous he became muddled and forgetful. They talked for over an hour and bit by bit Johannes relaxed. By the time they were done, he had dropped his self-protective posture; he no longer suffered from feeling continually judged. As soon as his attitude changed, he began to pick up tricks from others at work. Once he was given the opportunity—by Steve's willingness to reach out to him—to reveal his true self, he could accept and act upon a vision of himself as something other than a bumbling idiot. In this case, as in Carolyn's, Compassion proved to be a healing force.

Helping People Help Themselves

There is a subtle shadow side of Compassion, and that is dysfunctional rescuing. By this I mean playing nice, giving superficial pity, taking on another person's anxiety, or trying to solve somebody's problems for them. One of the most fulfilling experiences in life is discovering unique solutions for our own problems; when we engage in dysfunctional rescuing we are denying the person we are seeking to help this empowering step.

In my own community, as in all groups where Compassion is valued, we are all helpers. But not all "help" is helpful. Some approaches to helping can be quite dysfunctional for ourselves and for others. Alcoholics Anonymous teaches that there is a form of help that actually enables another's addiction rather than helping the addicted person come to terms with the disease-oriented nature of addiction and find effective treatment. Equally, functional Compassion is not about solving people's problems for them, but helping them solve those problems themselves. A distraught woman approached one of my mentors, the priest Henry Hudson, at his church one day, seeking an answer to a personal quandary. She pleaded with him to tell her exactly what to do. Instead, he explored options with her, gave her referral information for therapists and other medical personnel, and reviewed spiritual disciplines that would be important to engage. Then he said, "I will be very interested to know what you and God work out as your plan." He understood that in order to really extend Compassion, he had to put the power to find a solution in her hands.

A few years ago, I traveled to South Africa for work. Two friends picked me up in Cape Town and drove me along the gleaming freeway and then several dusty, unpaved roads to the tip of the continent for an overnight visit in a tiny fishing village. A group of us sat together in a mud-baked building with small windows, eating fried fish that had been caught that day. With us were several women who had lost their fishermen husbands in sea accidents. Poor, of color, widowed, they had had no visible means of support.

My friends had spent time listening to the grief of these women as a part of their work in the nonprofit organization HOPE Africa. They also had paid attention to their hopes. They noticed seeds of self-sufficiency. Some widows were talented cooks. Others were clever craftswomen. Yet others had unrealized abilities in business and accounting. My friends brought in volunteers from Cape Town who taught the widows skills in computing, accounting, and running a business. Now these women support themselves in a modest cottage business for tourists.

This experience revealed to me the essence of functional helping as opposed to dysfunctional rescuing. My friends called their work "people-centered economic development." Too frequently, they explained, Western visitors encounter poverty-rooted pain and want to apply a rapid solution to alleviate that pain—both the pain they are witnessing and the pain activated within themselves. So the visitors apply solutions that reflect a Western mentality, such as creating a one-time project supplying money and technology; this has more to do with themselves than with the hopes and dreams of the people suffering. Such solutions, which come from the imagination of the observers more than the imagination of the sufferers, fall flat and cannot be sustained over the long haul. Front and center in those activities are the feelings of the helper, not the helped. They often reek of arrogance and condescension.

Because they didn't come from quality time spent getting to know the person in need, they almost never are, as Galway Kinnell wrote in the poem that opens this chapter, a hand on the brow, reteaching someone their loveliness until they flower again from within. Compassion is about recognizing someone's essential humanity and thereby allowing them to grow and heal.

The Moral Self

Those who practice the Habit of Compassion are not in denial about a horrendous act someone has done. There is no denying that human beings can do evil and destructive things to the innocent and the vulnerable. Nor does it mean that we can go about our daily tasks without encountering people who act less respectfully toward others and our collective civic life than we do. We cannot avoid contact with "mean" people or fear-entrenched or fear-mongering types. And sadly, none of us can be fully protected from those who practice violence. However, we can remember, through practice, that there is a latent loveliness inherent in every human being— even those in whom goodness is heavily disguised. To the degree that I am free from fear and allow love to flow through me, I can practice love in all my relationships *no matter what*. This is a concept I first heard from Father Greg.

Part of being Compassionate is insisting on a system of laws based on accountability, short of the death penalty. However, at the center of holding someone accountable, even if it may involve life in prison without parole, is the understanding that in every human being there is a loving self that we—and they—may not have access to, but that is never entirely wiped out.

Both war and the death penalty, for example, are often justified by fear-based classifications of certain people as "monsters." That ignores the sacred goodness in every human, and provides a fallacious rationale for killing them. As soon as we insist that someone is less than human, we make ourselves less than human. There is something about hate and the studied refusal to be Compassionate toward our enemies that distorts our own personality.

In a rule-of-law mentality, justice is seen as "truth discovery." The disarray is put back in order through compensation or, if need be, punishments such as imprisonment. This is restorative justice. However, in a rule-of-war mentality, justice is seen as meting out an eye-for-an-eye retribution—which Gandhi noted leaves the whole

world blind. If someone is killed, there has to be a resulting and pro-
portionate death, which in reality is rarely kept to the boundaries of
proportionality. This is retributive justice.

Restorative justice frees a person or people to move forward with
sober wisdom and sincere efforts to interrupt the spiral of violence
and make effective investments in restoring wholeness. The latter
sentences the person or people to revisit or even reenact the original
offense ad infinitum with escalating acts of violence.

It is the role of those who were hurt, and their allies, to find
ways to stop the spiral of aggression before it leads to brutality and
even more bloodshed. The energy field of fear cannot accomplish
this goal. Only the energy field of love has the capacity to establish
peace.

Our loving self, from the perspective of this book, is exhibited
when we take crimes against humanity to court rather than to war
or to assassination. When Colonel Muammar Gaddafi of Libya was
captured and killed in 2011, a Libyan attorney said of those who
took him prisoner and then brutally murdered him, "They could
not access their moral self."

What an insightful commentary, which for me relates to the
Habit of Compassion. The moral self the lawyer was talking about
is merely another name for the loving self. Acting as they did with
no Compassion for this man who caused them so much pain mir-
rored Gaddafi's fearful self back to him in his last moments on earth.
Treating him with Compassion, on the other hand, would have
brought him, intact, to a court of law, and also kept open to him the
reality of the loving nature present in all humankind, which he had
denied to terrible effect throughout his own life.

How to Practice Compassion

The Habit of Compassion is, at its core, about acting on the knowledge that everyone is a God carrier in our everyday lives—including

ourselves. Practicing Compassion means bringing a person or group with whom we disagree or who have done us wrong back into the fold of a loving humanity. It challenges us to continually look beyond ourselves and extend love to all members of the human family, regardless of what they may have done in the past. It distinguishes between charitable empathy in which we seek to simply wipe out others' pain or discomfort, and incites us to action in which we honor their future by helping them help and honor themselves. The Habit of Compassion reminds us that none of us is as evil as our worst act; no evil deed or deeds can erase the goodness and love at our core.

While Compassion may not come easily to all of us, especially when we are hurt or horrified, we can learn to incorporate it into our daily actions. You do not have to embrace it all at once; all that matters is that you take the next step forward. Simply desiring to come to a place where you want to extend the energy of Compassion to others, overcoming the resistances and rationalizations of your fearful self, is to stay on the journey of Compassion, leaving the stranglehold of fear behind.

❋ Take a moment for Stillness, to remember when you have been on the receiving end of Compassion. In the quiet, let come into your mind a time when someone saw in you a special gift or way of being in the world. When I allow myself to practice such a meditation, my mind visits all the different periods of my life. For some of us such a moment has happened quite recently. For others it may have happened in our childhood. For me it was the lady who watched me during the day when I was a child and both my parents were working.

❋ If after several minutes you have not rested on a single event, open yourself to the Beloved or the spirit of the universe or your higher power (however you may think about ultimate power). Ask that Compassionate One to give you a sense of the goodness and beauty residing in your core that has been there since you were born. Perhaps then you will see those moments in your life when Compassion was extended to you, and this will release in you the desire to extend that Compassion to others and complete the circle of love.

* Participate in an activity that results in self-blessing; as the opening poem says, we are seeking the patient flowering again from within the gift of self-blessing. This may happen as you walk through the echoing halls of an art gallery, gazing upon the paintings. Perhaps music unleashes the caring spirit within you or dancing brings you to a place of joy, and you can then extend this feeling to others. Perhaps watching a child's face as he or she laughs reminds you of your own blessings.

* If these steps do not take place immediately, do not be frustrated. Sometimes it takes a while. Each year I go on an eight-day silent retreat. The first day is spent praying in such a way to bring to mind how deeply and unconditionally loved we are. If it doesn't happen in one day, then the retreat director doesn't proceed with the remainder of the retreat. For you, perhaps you will need an afternoon of soul searching, a day away from your responsibilities, a long-awaited vacation with loved ones. Or perhaps it will take a more consistent effort over weeks and months, but with each day you will be taking a step toward finding what makes your soul blossom.

* With the confidence that you, too, are Beloved, it is time to extend that to others. Start with those close to you. Imagine them as needing to be reminded of the goodness dwelling in the core of their being. Send to them the energy that you feel when you are accessing your own moral self, your own loved and loving self, your own unique self. Extend this Compassion to those in your larger orbit of family, friends, and colleagues.

* Many of us do not find these steps so difficult. Where the real challenge lies is being Compassionate to those we have dismissed as

unworthy, inhuman, or simply bad. Bring to mind those with whom you have persistent difficulty or those upon whom you pass harsh judgment. Imagine that they are people created by the same power of love that created you. Imagine that there is a core of goodness in them and the reason they have not expressed that goodness toward you is because of some story line or conceptual model for the world that someone of power told them they were to live by. That fearful story has resulted in their not being able to love others compassionately. Send to them the energy you have felt when you have returned to your loving self. You will feel tension draining from your body; those negative and fearful feelings you have been harboring weigh heavily on your heart.

🌸 When seeking to practice functional Compassion, remember to always see the individuals as people with hopes and dreams for their lives, for their family's lives, and for the life of their community. This is not about you unburdening your feelings of pity, but about extending Generosity, the very first Habit of Love we explored, in constructive ways. That is why, for instance, when I give money to provide relief in the face of disasters like famines and earthquakes, I always give to an organization that does two things: first, provides effective immediate relief, and second, commits to an ongoing relationship with people. Relief and development organizations that try to learn what the peoples' hopes and dreams are will be part of making those hopes and dreams come true so the survivors of a disaster can discover their own power.

🌸 Part of the responsibility of being a leader in a family, business, faith community, or any other system lies in responding to difficult personalities with firm and gentle Compassion. Though I have spent hours imagining the core of goodness in other persons, I have also periodically had to talk with someone else—perhaps a spiritual counselor, or on certain occasions, a therapist—about my occasional difficulty extending compassionate energy toward another person. Sarah, an exemplary and courageous leader in my own faith community, once told me that she was so infuriated at another member of our church that she called her therapist for extra sessions just to deal with her anger. It made all the difference in Sarah (not in the difficult person), and that was enough. Sarah has understood that practicing Compassion means not only drawing on her loving self when dealing with others, but also sharing that love with the world. We cannot withhold Compassion from another without withholding it from ourselves. William Slone Coffin said of the Romans who crucified Jesus, "They could not have crucified the best among us without first crucifying the best in themselves." Each of us is that interconnected in the human community.

CHAPTER EIGHT

The Habit of Community

No man is an island, entire of itself; every man is
a piece of the continent, a part of the main...Any
man's death diminishes me, because I am involved in mankind, and therefore never send to
know for whom the bell tolls; it tolls for thee.

—John Donne

While you have probably heard the expression "we live alone and
we die alone," neither of those statements is true. You cannot be a
human being alone. You cannot be healthy alone; you cannot heal
alone; you cannot flourish alone; you cannot cast off fear alone; you
cannot be a lover alone; and you cannot access the Beloved inside
you and inside other people alone. Understood from this perspective, we are not the human race, we are the human family.

The Habit of Community lets us know that we are not, in fact,
alone. Each of the other seven Habits of Love ultimately leads to
this most critical, life-affirming habit. Community conquers fear
in a way that no other habit does: it counters the central fear—
perhaps our very deepest fear—that we are essentially alone in the
world.

Some years ago, a young woman named Liz and her husband,
Matt, were expecting their first baby. The pregnancy was tough—

almost unbearable morning sickness for months on end along with complications that led to bed rest at home for a few weeks and then in the hospital. Thrilled at the prospect of starting a family together, and far from their families back in Minnesota, Matt started a blog to keep everyone updated. On March 24 he posted pictures of a tiny baby girl weighing almost four pounds and a picture of a happy and exhausted Liz, lying in her hospital bed, blond hair pulled back, cooing at her infant as the baby was taken to the NICU. Madeline Logelin had arrived, weeks early but doing well.

The next post was not the next day, nor the next. It was four days later, and it was an obituary for Liz. On March 25, as she was preparing to go see Maddy for the first time after the birth, she suffered a pulmonary embolism and died instantly. Matt was on his own, a father and then a widower in the space of 27 hours.

Then over the next few weeks an extraordinary thing happened: Matt accidentally discovered a new Community that offered him hope. They never met in person, yet these strangers gave him support—both psychological and practical—during a time of unparalleled sorrow. In the middle of the night, after a long feeding or a messy diaper change, Matt began to tell his story to the invisible readers of his blog. He wrote about Liz. He wrote about the baby. He asked for advice. And he began to hear back. Soon thousands and thousands of mothers were reaching out to him. While each day was a struggle, he was not in this struggle alone. "This outpouring of advice and kindness was yet another demonstration of the power of community, and of community as extended family," he wrote, "...because I didn't belong to a church or any neighborhood groups, there was no organized effort to assist us. Nevertheless, I'd stumbled into these sympathetic individuals online."

We all need Community, in whatever form we find or create it, to give us courage, inspire us to change, and hold us accountable. We cannot make it through hard times alone, nor do we wish to experience the good times alone either. Sharing our pain and our joy with others helps us turn away from the bleakness of our fearful nature, and embrace the loved and loving self that is always within us, no matter how dire our situation is. Community helps us access our open-hearted selves. In isolation, we are but one small grain of sand that can easily be washed away. In our chosen Community, we become instead a rock that has the power to stand up to the strong currents of the ocean.

I Am Because We Are

The organizers of my high school class reunion in Georgia once asked me to be the speaker at our Reunion Banquet. That's a tough assignment—these people "knew you when," as the saying goes. I had changed so much since being a teenager, and had been living for many years at a great distance geographically from my former classmates. Could I find a way to bridge the distance between us? What could I possibly say that would be of any help or inspiration? The morning of the speech I went to work out in the town fitness center to find some peace and think over what I might say to my old friends. Over the rack of free weights a small poster caught my eye:

DO NOT USE HEAVY WEIGHTS WITHOUT A SPOTTER
PERMANENT INJURIES MAY OCCUR

The Beloved gave me my speech in that poster. That evening I spoke about how I had enjoyed some victories in high school and, like most others gathered around me listening with upturned faces, I had also faced some painful challenges. But the experience had left no permanent scars on me because of the sheer number of friends and teachers who were just like "spotters" in a gym. When they saw me struggling with a hefty weight, they would come and stand over me or behind me with their hands right under the weights. If the weights slipped from my shaky grip, these spotters were ready to ease them back to the floor instead of letting them drop onto my body. That is the power of Community: it lets us know that we are never truly alone, however much we may be suffering or battling our fears.

In Hawaii, it has become common to use the word *aloha* as an expression of greeting, as though it means simply "hello." But the word's cultural roots grew from something more elaborate. In the past, when two natives greeted one another they would "come together" (*alo*), touch their foreheads together, and then breathe in one another's spirit or life force (*ha* means "breath" or "life"). So in its original form *aloha* means "coming together to take in another person's spirit or breath or life." This is what Matt's online Community did for him in those months and years after his wife's death and his baby's birth: it shared in and perpetuated his life spirit, and passed its spirit on to him through words on the screen.

Archbishop Desmond Tutu says something similar in describing the Zulu word *ubuntu*. He translates *ubuntu* as "a person is a person through other persons." The archbishop explains that in those African cultures where the word *ubuntu* is a part of the native tongue, people say that you can know and feel when someone is "carrying ubuntu inside them"—when someone is living life in the spirit of ubuntu. These concepts of Community, aloha, and ubuntu are embraced by those who know it is not the case that "I think, therefore I am." Rather, the truth is, "I am because we are."

This "I am" includes my never-ending transformation, because I am in Community with others. I am not evolved enough to carry around within myself consistent impartiality, fairness, justice, courage, and open-hearted and serene states of being. These values can be found where the spirit of Community thrives—where people know and feel their unceasing connectedness.

I can think, create, imagine, care for my young, and show Compassion to others, even my adversaries and enemies, because I know and feel that we are all caught up in and given life and energy by the Beloved. Dr. Martin Luther King described this orientation toward life when he explained that whatever affects one person directly impacts all others indirectly. He explained that he could not reach his goals and be what he was meant to be until others are able to do the same, and vice versa. We all have a responsibility to do our work and live our lives in such a way that we become who we were meant to be, but we do that work and live that life with the consciousness of Community—and so, concurrently, we have a responsibility to help others so they may become who they are meant to be as well.

It's Not about Numbers

Community is not just a collection of individuals, it is a coming together of people who work constantly to cast aside their fearful selves and open their hearts to allow the Beloved within to flow outward toward others, perpetuating the inflow and outflow of energy as we discussed in the Habit of Generosity. Community does not have to include a cast of thousands. The experience of one young woman named Carrie Ryan, who was recently invited to attend Oxford University on a Rhodes Scholarship, reveals how she inadvertently created a Community of two.

Each weekend when she was a high school student, Carrie visited her grandfather at the nursing home where he lived. She began to notice a pattern each time she arrived: an elderly man would be sitting by the front door in a folding chair, alone. He was always there when she arrived, and he was always there when she left. The nurses told her he only took a break from his watch at the door to eat his meals or sleep for a few hours. Two years earlier, John's family had dropped him off at the home, never to return. So eager was he for the Community of family, he parked himself at the driveway like a sentinel so as to be certain not to miss their arrival. Day after day, week after week, they did not come.

While Carrie's grandfather took his nap, she got into the pattern of going downstairs to sit with John. That summer, she visited the nursing home every day, and she always spent some time sitting and talking with her new friend. He would tell her about his life: about his rug business, his career in the military, his first crush, and the only love of his life, his wife. They became very close. But one day when she came to visit, John was not sitting at the door.

His heart medicine was no longer working as it should, the nurses explained. Today might be his last day.

Carrie rushed to his room, pulling up a chair to his bedside. He reached out for her and they clasped hands. "I knew his family would not show up and I wanted to be there for him," she said. After an hour the heart monitor went off and the nurses rushed in; still holding his hand, Carrie began to cry. "In that moment John passed, something stirred up inside of me...I knew John, I loved John, and I saw John die alone, without his family."

Without even knowing it, Carrie was practicing the Habit of Community. Throughout John's last few months, she was giving this stranger the companionship and love he had been waiting for. In the end, he died knowing he was not alone. Community is not always about numbers: it is about intention, acknowledgment, and listening to someone when they need to "tell."

We come together to tell our stories because it takes us from a place of fear where we live in isolation to a place of Community where we are never truly alone. A child in therapy feels she is being heard and understood, and, in gaining insights into herself through sharing, no longer has anxiety attacks on her way to school. A widow in a bereavement group gathers courage from knowing others, too, have suffered as she does and have lived to tell. The guests at a wedding participate in the moment of joy, but also commit to becoming part of an ongoing Community that will celebrate and uphold the values of the couple whose union they are witnessing. Funerals allow mourners to breathe life once again into the deceased, calling up their spirit by sharing stories with friends. It is always remarkable how often funerals turn into occasions of boisterous laughter and delight. Sometimes a sense of elation can even come over the attendees. Why is this? Because interactions with

Community feed and delight our souls, bringing the Beloved to the fore.

I have known this Community energy when in the presence of just one friend, and in the presence of many. I could not do what I do in life without my wife, our children Peter and Alice, our grandchildren, my friends, my colleagues, and my worshipping community. Each of these Communities has transformed my life. During the writing of this book when I was occasionally away from my Community for weeks at a time, I still attended church each week—not out of a sense of duty, but because I feel refreshed from being in the midst of people who are working together to become less fearful.

All along, what matters is that we are not trying to be who we are alone. What is required is to reach out and say, "I need a spotter. I need a Community. You and I really need one another."

There Are No Strangers

In 1958, the Trappist monk and author Thomas Merton was in Louisville, Kentucky, walking in town after having visited the doctor for a routine appointment. Shortly, he would be returning to his monastery deep in the Kentucky countryside. As he was strolling along Walnut Street (now renamed Muhammad Ali Boulevard), Merton experienced a flash of enlightenment that was to define the rest of his life. Looking around him at the young and old in the streets of that city, he later wrote, "I was suddenly overwhelmed with the realization that I loved these people, that they were mine and I theirs, that we could not be alien to one another even though we were total strangers...I suddenly saw the secret beauty of their hearts, the depths of their hearts where neither sin nor desire nor self-knowledge can reach, the core of their reality, the person that each one is in God's eyes."

As a monk, he had been living the notion of "separation from the world." He called this self-isolation "a complete illusion," a dream from which he later awoke. His epiphany in that moment was that a separate life of renunciation obscured the beauty and power of Community. He said it was a misconception that: "by making vows we become a different species of being, pseudoangels 'spiritual men'...but does that entitle us to consider ourselves different, or even better than others? The whole idea is preposterous."

While Merton's stunning insight is one that some of us feel intuitively, a good number of us find it alien because we do not feel a deep connectedness with all human beings. Many of us have been in situations in which we are surrounded by people, and yet feel utterly alone. It might be in our families, where we feel misunderstood; in our work, where we are not being heard; or in our social circles, where others are not reflecting our values. Perhaps we are simply too embroiled in our own concerns to open ourselves up, making ourselves vulnerable, to others. Perhaps we feel the fear of scarcity and we prefer to look out for ourselves alone.

We need only look around us at the business practices that have become acceptable over the past few decades to see how far from the spirit of Community a group of people can get. The recent banking scandals are a prime example of this. The desire for accumulation of wealth often overwhelms our sense of responsibility toward and kinship with others; the pursuit of profits trumps providing for public needs in health care and education. But when we act from our loving selves, the affinity between every individual becomes clear and guides us in our behavior. As Merton wrote of those ordinary folks he saw that day, "If only they could all see themselves as they really are. If only we could see each other that way all the time. There would be no more war, no more hatred, no more cruelty, no more greed."

On the streets of Los Angeles and Pasadena I often encounter persons who are homeless, many of whom are mentally ill. Merton's "Louisville Epiphany" invariably comes to my mind at those times. When it does, I am able to relate to an unknown homeless person on the street as someone who is not alien to me, no matter how different our lives, or way of thinking, may be. In the words of Merton, "They are mine and I am theirs."

The dynamic of Community happens when a shift takes place in our consciousness and we welcome into our awareness the existence of this web of life. It would benefit our nation greatly if we could build into our culture a period of time when everyone serves the public good. Friends who have worked in the Peace Corps or Americorps have without fail expressed to me how deeply the experience impacted their lives by shifting their awareness and appreciation of others in a profoundly positive way. Galvanizing and eye-opening, these service experiences should become part of the fabric of our lives. Everyone benefits from giving of their time and energy to the building of a healthy Community, and it is our responsibility to help young people recognize this symbiotic relationship. Thankfully, many schools and families appreciate the importance of building commitment to Community into their everyday routines. So much of modern life is fragmented and frenzied that we become dehumanized. Working together to create Community counters this fragmentation and restores us to our humanity. When we live our daily lives based on the awareness that we all share spiritual and moral kinship, we are practicing the Habit of Community. We truly become not just the human race but the human *family*.

The Need to Be Heard

Dan Nigro was the chief operations officer of the New York City Fire Department when he drove across the Brooklyn Bridge on the morning of September 11, 2001. He lived to tell his story, and to pay witness to the stories of others. Amid the tales of horror and fear, powerful tales of courage and Community emerged. A city whose residents are infamous for their individualistic approach to life was permanently transformed that day by the power of the spontaneous Communities that sprang up—and that continue to bring strength to survivors more than a decade after the attacks.

Nigro attended hundreds of funerals for firefighters who were killed when the Twin Towers crumbled. "You saw these kids who had lost their fathers, mothers who had lost their sons, and I always tried to feel that I was a sponge that would absorb everyone's grief," he recounted. "I can't believe that all these people were church-going folk, but I think everyone's spirituality grew during this period."

I tell this story not simply to highlight how, in times of crisis, we pull together. I tell it because when humans are in pain it is our instinct to mourn together, looking for explanations by turning to a higher power. I tell it because Nigro took the instinct for Community a step further and practiced this habit long after the events of that traumatic day were over. His father, an old firefighter, advised him to visit each one of the 90 firehouses in the surrounding area that had lost people in the attack. Week after week, Nigro stopped by one or two of the stations on his way home after work. Sometimes the visits were short and straightforward, an acknowledgment of the firefighters' experiences, whether shared or unique. Sometimes they were longer and more challenging as Nigro—who had been pro-moted to Fire Department chief after the former chief, Peter Ganci, was killed on 9/11—listened to their words and shared in their anger and fear.

His father was right: healing words had to be spoken. That year of listening proved to be so transformational for Nigro that he finds it hard to recall the hundreds of fires and countless career milestones he experienced in all the preceding decades. Like Merton, his life was forevermore divided into *before* and *after*.

In moments of terror—or simply embarrassment—fear tempts us to isolate. Isolation fuels our fantasy life. Negative fantasies fed by our fear that things are going horribly wrong, or that no one cares, or that we are screwups, grow wildly in the petri dish of isolation.

Talking initiates Community. Even a simple call to a supportive, compassionate person just to hear his or her voice can alter one's day for the better. Voices have vibrational frequencies that register in our brains, bodies, and spirits. Feeling the vibrations of a compassionate being can dispel the negativity that fear in isolation causes.

The Courage to Tell

One of my parishioners, Cathy, is a cancer survivor. To look at Cathy is to feel an internal warmth. Even when thinking of Cathy Clement, I smile. Over 60 years of age, mother of two adult children, grandmother of three, Cathy carries her tall, ballerina-thin frame with a smiling, chin-up, approachable confidence. Her walk is that of a dancer, toes pointed outward in fashionable high heels, moving with a definite destination in mind but not so driven that she is intimidating. After chemotherapy left her bald, Cathy grew her hair back in a short blond style, which made her even more striking. Her looks, however, are not the source of her inspiration. That comes from some stirring energy alive and active in her core that has overcome some defining battles with fear.

The afternoon that Cathy's doctor discovered the lymphoma, she returned home and immediately turned on her computer. "I'm going to tell," she wrote in a long email that became the first of an extended series of communications to more than 50 friends. She knew instinctively that she did not want to take this journey alone, and that she did not have to.

This phrase, "I'm going to tell," reminds me of a childhood saying. Whenever a bully cornered some poor kid, one of our threats was, "I'm going to tell." It meant, of course, we were going to tell a grown-up—someone with more power than we had who would stop the bullying. Cathy was telling her Community that a bully named Cancer was beating her up. All the Beloved energy within those per-

sons focused their energy on her so that she would get better. That
way, in addition to receiving grueling chemotherapy, Cathy also received the healing therapy of her Community's energy.

Later, cancer invaded my own home. When it came, I had
Cathy's spirit in my heart as inspiration.

A bump was growing in the center of my wife Hope's lower lip.
It was squamous cell carcinoma. As a professional speech patholo-
gist whose daily work involves using her lips to model how words
are spoken, it seemed a cruel irony that she was afflicted with this
cancer. How does a speech therapist teach a child to make the "p"
sound correctly if she can no longer make it that way herself? The
lump was growing quite rapidly, so we scheduled surgery as soon as
possible. Not only did this threaten Hope personally but also professionally. With this double threat in mind and remembering Cathy,
I gained Hope's permission to tell.

As soon as I "told" through emails and phone calls, Hope began
receiving cards, emails, phone calls, even a special message from
Archbishop Tutu. They all said that they would be praying for her.
It was as if our home was turned into a center for healing.

The day of her surgery, I drove Hope to the doctor's office. He cut
the circle-shaped muscle that allows us to purse our lips for kissing,
for forming some words, and for performing certain eating functions. A chunk of her lower lip was removed. After the doctor made
his first incision, I waited with Hope in the surgery room as he tested
the tissue. The memory of the sight I encountered still challenges
me. There was the love of my life, reclining in a surgical chair with
her bottom lip held open in a V-shape of pink severed flesh, vulner-
ably exposed.

I approached silently to touch her hand; she grasped mine in
response. Later when I asked what she had been thinking, she explained, "I was trying to let in all those prayers that people were
saying for me." She opened herself to receive the Community's
healing energy of love. That summer, our daughter and grand-
daughter came to be with us, as well as Hope's best friend, Ann. It

became a season of healing more than one of illness or grief. That is the point of the Habit of Community: it accesses the empowering, transformative energy that is ours in Creation's network of mutuality. We both give and receive that energy in a mutual exchange of healing and wholeness.

No one knows with certainty what determines our state of sickness or wellness or what helps us stave off a threat like cancer. But what I do know for certain is that there is power in bringing the energy of Community to bear on fighting the destructive energy of fear that visits us every time we are threatened.

Shining Light into the Darkness

On the outskirts of Kandahar, Afghanistan, you will find the Mirwais Mena School for Girls, a two-story cement structure encircled by high cement walls to protect the students inside. This school, one of only a few for girls in the entire country, is located about 20 miles from the hometown of Mullah Mohammed Omar, the founder of the Taliban.

Here, in the heart of the Taliban-controlled area, two teenage sisters, Shamsia and Atifa Husseini, were walking to school one morning. Black scarves covered most of their faces. Three motorcycles drove near the girls, each carrying two masked men. They buzzed ominously around the schoolgirls for several minutes. Then one of the cycles pulled alongside Shamsia, and the man on back jumped off while the driver idled. Speaking through his mask, he asked her, "Are you going to school?"

The masked man then yanked the scarf away from Shamsia's face and, with his other hand, pumped the trigger on a spray gun he had pulled from his satchel. The gun was filled with battery acid; instantly it seared through the layers of skin on her face. The girls screamed and Shamsia clutched her face in agony; Atifa tried to run away but was caught and sprayed on her back with the acid. The men raced off toward another group of girls, leaving Shamsia lying in the street.

Mahmood Qadri, the headmaster of the Mirwais Mena School for Girls, shuttered its doors after the acid attacks, but only for a week. Soon it was crowded and filled with the laughter and chatter of three hundred girls. Nearly all of the 11 girls and four teachers who were burned by battery acid that morning had returned. Most surprising was Shamsia Husseini. She was not only in attendance at the school again, but animated and lively, seated in the front row of her geography class. A blotchy scarlet scar covered the side of her face.

When asked about her return to school she exhibited a perfect grasp of the situation, both hers and her country's. "The people who did this to me don't want women to be educated. They want us to be stupid things."

Qadri went to the leaders of Kandahar Province and secured promises for a school bus, a team of police officers, and a walkway over the national highway outside. Then he called a meeting of the parents. "I told them, if you don't send your daughters to school, then the enemy wins," he said. "I told them not to give in to darkness."

Something had happened to Qadri's fear. Could it have been the power of Community empowering the girls, their parents, the headmaster, and, through reading this story, you and me as well? Each one of us has been transformed, in small ways and large, by the story of this hardscrabble Community of girls in Afghanistan.

The darkness the headmaster referred to is the darkness of a fear-based culture, whether that culture is found in Kandahar or Kansas. Wherever cultural norms keep an identified class of people demeaned, diminished, and dehumanized, that culture is based in fear. We saw it in action in the early days of desegregation, when white Americans were afraid to share their classrooms with African Americans—afraid to upend our outdated and unjust understanding of social order. We saw it when the Episcopal Church was asked to allow women to be ordained as priests, threatening the patriarchal underpinnings of an ancient institution. And, most recently, we see it in the struggle of gays and lesbians to be accorded the right to marry, which challenges old paradigms of love between a man and a woman.

Fear is working behind the scenes whenever privilege and discrimination fights with ganglike ferocity. Any effort to try to limit divine power only to "my kind of people"—whether it's men or Christians or white people or heterosexual folk—is an action based in the darkness of dread. The issue is whether or not we give into that darkness, whether we forget the Beloved's true work on the planet and inside of ourselves, or whether we remember, with each other's help, through Community.

Shamsia's story is shot through with the powerful, liberating energy of the Habit of Community. Other students and their families and certainly the headmaster invested their own love-based thinking in the Habit of Community so that together, they would not give in to darkness.

The Danger of Herd Mentality

People need Community to know they are not alone, but when this need is born from fear rather than love it can be dangerous. As we noted in the Habit of Compassion, a group is actually nothing more than a gang when its members are afraid that they may be cast out of that group if they don't think the way everyone else does. One of the most extreme examples of this in today's society can be found in cults—yet, while we may recognize groups that demand a dangerous level of adherence from its supporters, we often do not recognize when we ourselves are thinking in cultish ways. The most well-intentioned, sophisticated, humanistic, and even spiritual groups can inadvertently adopt this kind of behavior.

My friend Nell told me a story about an experience she had during college. A male student had been on a date with a friend, downing beers and shots of tequila. There was an altercation at the end of a long and drunken night, and the young man was accused of date rape. Stories about what happened soon hit the campus papers and the local media. Everyone had an opinion on the matter. For many, it seemed obvious the man was guilty; for others, it was obvious the woman was exaggerating, that it was wrong to call what happened "rape." The case went to trial. After a lengthy deliberation, it was determined that there was insufficient evidence to conclude the encounter had indeed been rape, and the young man was exonerated.

When word of the verdict got around, a group of feminists organized a protest. They taped flyers with the man's face printed on them onto trees all around campus; hundreds of enraged young people—mostly women—gathered together to march. Feelings were running high: the assembled group yelled and chanted, raised their fists in anger. They called out the name of the accused, again and again, insisting on his guilt.

At first Nell joined in. There was an assumed bond between these women. In this instance, that bond was strengthened by the emotions of the gathering crowd, and those emotions grew as the crowd swelled.

But a friend of Nell's had doubts. "You know," she said anxiously, looking around her at the fuming faces, "we probably don't know the full story."

Nell began to feel uncomfortable. Here she was, shouting this man's name, possibly doing him damage. Was she protesting the supposed crime? The accused himself? Or was she protesting the ruling that had cleared his name? The adjudication process had been lengthy and careful. Nell realized she was making assumptions, getting carried away in the spirit of the moment, and that facts and feelings had become confused. This is the herd mentality at work: Nell had, in a sense, "outsourced" her thinking. When Community is exclusionary or judgmental, it can wield power that is harmful.

Family dynamics can operate in similar ways. We yearn for the approval of our parents, fearing we will be cast out if we do not share their exact values or ideology. The Hultgrens are a close extended family that spends most Sunday afternoons together sharing a long lunch. They'll sit around the dining room table for hours, talking and eating. In the past, the discussions often revolved around politics and became heated. One or another of the four grown children and their spouses was constantly in and out of favor with the parents and each other when one of them disagreed with the others. Lunches became so contentious and relationships so frayed that they decided to put a moratorium on talking about politics.

But Community is not about conformism; true Community tolerates and even celebrates divergent opinions and personalities. When a cooperative group of independent thinkers come together to enjoy and affirm their differences rather than be in and out of favor over disagreements, this makes for a healthy Community. Only when the Hultgrens manage to find a way to agree to disagree—to let go of the fear that makes it hard for them to accept each other's divergent opinions—will they truly become a resilient, nourishing, and healthy Community.

Community Embraces Differences

As a priest, I have learned to always ask myself and others, To what degree is a position of theological orthodoxy in fact the result of herd thinking? To what degree does membership in this group require outsourcing my thinking to accepted conventions? I have also come to suspect that a great deal of orthodoxy is rooted in fear.

One evening I was facilitating a Bible study in one of the churches where I have served. We were deep in discussion when Jim's face reddened and he began a rant against homosexuals "gaining power in the church." He pointed to the Bible as proof of his position, going on at length with the "orthodox" argument that the

Bible is "against homosexuality." In listening to him that night, it struck me that his language seemed to be coming from his fear of something intangible; it was not the vocabulary he usually used. It seemed like an argument written by another person.

"Jim, I couldn't disagree with you more," another member of the group, Jenny, stated, kindly and matter-of-factly. She was using the Habit of Candor. Then she told of her brother-in-law who is gay and who is also a devout Christian and lives in a life-giving, long-term relationship with another man. "I hear all your scriptural arguments, Jim. It's just that I cannot believe that my brother-in-law is either unnatural or an abomination," Jenny continued. "He is one of us— just as much a part of the human community as you and I are. And I believe he is loved just as he is, as much as you and Esther and Bill and I are in our marriages."

The way Jenny said it was liberating for everyone sitting around that table. Of course it didn't convert Jim to her perspective; she hadn't infused her objection with that intention. She was simply gently expressing a conviction to which Truth had led her. The gift of her statement for that group was that everyone felt encouraged to find their own voice in this experience of Community. An energy grew in the discussion that seemed to be giving everyone license to disagree as well as agree, to put forward their own arguments from both everyday life and from religious tradition.

Rather than exhibiting herd mentality, true Community, I find, encourages everyone to clarify their own values without having to agree with the group. There are few experiences that bring more energy to the soul than belonging to a durable Community without the pressure of having to agree.

The Power of "The House"

I have a lifetime of experience with gatherings of people, whether it is the gathering of a faith community for worship, friends for an evening of theater, or people for a lecture, speech, or rock concert. Every gathering has its own energy. I learned this as the son of a clergyman, growing up going to church twice each Sunday and every Wednesday night. Any given gathering of people has its own unique identity; each assembly feels different from another in great part because of the energy each person brings with them to the room or to the venue. Needless to say, the energy of the gathering can change during the course of the event because of other factors. But in this case I am speaking of the collective energy of the room as an event begins.

Actors frequently talk about how the "house" was. "It was a great house," they might say, or "It was a tough house." On the drive home from church, my preacher father would say, "The Spirit was strong at church this morning," or "The Spirit had a tough time getting through to us this evening." That phenomenon was always perplexing to me; as a boy I thought it had something to do with whether certain people had attended church or not that day. There were members of my father's congregations who were sweet, devoted, joyful, encouraging, and positive—and there were others whose own energy stew included pessimism, whining, destructive criticism, and the fear of anything other than the habitual. It was not until I read Alice Walker's novel *The Color Purple* that I had a clearer understanding of what made for a good "house" on a Sunday morning.

Shug Avery is the daughter of a Baptist preacher, and one of the central characters in the book. She is anything but a compliant church lady, having transformed all the intelligence, creativity, and spirit that she inherited from her father into becoming a woman of the world, the street, the honky-tonk bar. Shug has turned her back on the church, no longer attending services. She insists that the value of church lies not in the fact that people go on Sundays, but the value lies in what they bring with them when they go.

"Tell the truth, have you ever found God in church?" Shug asks. "I never did. I just found a bunch of folks waiting for him to show. Any God I ever felt in church I brought in with me. I think all the other folks did too. They come to church to share God, not find God."

When I read that passage, a light switched on for me. When we practice the Habits of Love in whatever form we encounter them, allowing the Beloved to transform us from our fearful selves into our loving selves, we transform a group of individuals into a Community. Like Matt Logelin, who inadvertently created a Community—just by *telling* in his blog—to which he could turn when fear of the future without his wife, Liz, paralyzed him. Like the teacher who, in practicing Compassion rather than acting in anger, can find common ground with difficult students. They become a team rather than opponents in a boxing ring. Or like the boss who, instead of separating herself from her co-workers, creates a dialogue in which everyone is free to express opinions and offer ideas. Through give and take, a Community is strengthened, fear is reduced, and each member of the Community becomes more connected to his or her open-hearted selves.

Thus we have to be able to *give* Community as well as *receive* it. I once overheard a yoga teacher tell one of his students, "Thank you for bringing your energy here today." That's what my father and millions of other religious leaders, actors, musicians, dancers, lecturers, teachers, and speakers have felt across the ages: gratitude for bringing the spirit of Community to others.

How to Practice Community

We are all on a lifelong journey away from isolation and herd thinking toward the warmth and power of Community. How would you tell your own story of that journey? When have you felt so different from others that you didn't share a sense of being a part of the human family? Have there been times when another person or some experience broke through that sense of isolation (as with Merton's illusion of separateness) and made you feel that you and others, especially those who are different, were actually connected? That belonging did not depend on acting and thinking like the other members of the group? That is the experience of Community.

My hope and belief is that everyone can experience the beauty and healing power of Community. By embodying love actively and engaging the Beloved within ourselves, we can conspire to transform the entire world into a love-based Community. The word *conspire* means "to breathe with"; surely this is a conspiracy to which we can all aspire.

* Make a conscious choice to spend time with people whose energy is loving and supportive, rather than exclusionary or moralistic. We have all had friends who take more than they give, who rain on our parade, who transmit their fear to us no matter how hard we try to deflect it. Take stock of how you relate to these people and extend Compassion. Perhaps the Habit of Candor can help you steer your relationship away from the negativity and toward positivity. It has been illuminating for me to notice how I gravitate to persons who have an energy about them that is more loving than fearful. They inspire my own desires to live a fear-free life. I think our deepest desires have to do with freedom. The desire of the Beloved for every human being is to be free. Persons who have committed themselves to practice the Habit of Community have influenced me to live each day of my life more freely.

* Become aware of people in your family, business, or social network who slot others into categories, with one group being favored over another. Conversely, are there persons in your life who tend to emphasize the interconnectedness of every human being? How does it feel to be in their presence? Does one or the other have a pronounced tendency to be fearful or loving? At the heart of ubuntu, the aloha spirit, and the Habit of Community is the fact that we cannot be our open-hearted selves alone. Who in your network of family,

friends, and associates can you count on to encourage your practicing the Habit of Community? Make sure that you are making time to be with them in your schedule—time for a conversation or a meal or even a retreat together.

* If you have yet to find a group where genuine Community is routinely employed to free oneself and others from fear, sincerely seek others who have and learn how Community is playing a role in their life. Does their Community attract you? If not, perhaps you are being called to gather a new group together. You can use this book as a starting point for discussions with others, perhaps in your local library, your congregation, or a coffee house. Move on to other books and resources. The goal is to deepen your understanding that "I am because we are."

* To some, the idea of Community is truly daunting. Perhaps you prefer the peace and quiet of your own thoughts. I would encourage you to find Community in other ways then: visiting art galleries, reading books, watching movies. Find opportunities to open yourself to the concerns, dreams, and philosophies of others. It will be spiritually enriching and allow you to become part of the greater world of thoughts and ideas. Additionally, joining an outdoor organization such as a hiking or running club will give you something to do other than focusing on making small talk. You may find a Community grows around you organically, without you having to try especially hard.

* For those of you who wish you had a stronger physical Community with others but feel socially awkward or shy, practice Stillness and allow yourself to see the inner strength that lies at your core. Trusting that the Beloved dwells within you may give you the ease you need to make those personal connections with others. Remember, too, that you are not alone in this sentiment. Many people feel just the way you do; it is time for you, and for them, to "tell" and share.

✳ Do you get the sense that your chosen Community is shunning you—that there is some divide you cannot figure out that keeps you from feeling the interconnectedness that people around you seem to be enjoying? Open yourself up to the Habit of Truth and the practice of Stillness and look deep inside, with as much objectivity as you can muster, to ask yourself if you have a role to play in turning people away. Examine, as honestly as possible, whether you may be judging or excluding others, and whether this has an impact on their judging or excluding you. If you cannot figure out what the reason is, experiment with the Habit of Generosity the next time you are in this Community, and see whether being giving and open to others might nudge the door open for you.

✳ If you are in a Community, whether it is formal or informal, ask yourself if this group gains its energy and status from being exclusionary or inclusionary. Does it insist on uniformity of thought or encourage members to think for themselves and have differences of opinion? Remember the story about our study group disagreeing about homosexuality? Your group does not have to always agree or always be harmonious, but your group can enjoy each member claiming the freedom to speak and live their own Truth without being excluded, respecting everyone's differences so that everyone can share the light of the Beloved.

A Final Note

It's the heart afraid of breaking
that never learns to dance.
It's the dream afraid of waking
That never takes a chance.
It's the one who won't be taken
Who cannot seem to give.
And the soul afraid of dying
That never learns to live.

—Amanda McBroom, "The Rose"

My Friend,

We have been on a journey together, but we have not reached the end—we have arrived at the beginning now. You see, the trajectory of pure love is always forward. The energy of unimpeded love neither holds onto the past nor tries to enshrine the present. It doesn't keep us on the safe side of the conventional, the proven, and the repetitious, but urges us to move forward. And so I urge you too, to take what you have learned in these pages, make it uniquely yours, and move forward in the spirit of love.

As I have said, though being open hearted is the most fulfilling way to live, it is not always the easiest way. At every turn, you will bump up against your fears. You will be hindered by that crippling energy that holds you back from living to your full potential, and helping others do the same. At times it will surely feel as though you do not have the fortitude, the will, or even the desire to break away. Perhaps you have lived with fear so long that it feels like home base for you; it's your default position in life. But love teaches us that we can—in fact, for our own sake and that of the world, we *must*—trust that love is stronger than fear. We must break free in order to live unimpeded and emancipated in the warm, blazing light of love.

Though the familiar may be causing us pain or holding us back, we often find comfort in it. It takes courage to step outside our comfort zone in order to embrace the unknown. "Let your courage rise with danger," is a mantra that guided Nelson Mandela through his decades as a prisoner on Robben Island and during the years afterward. Those words came from the first South African to win the Nobel Peace Prize, Chief Albert Luthuli. The 8 Habits of Love now call upon you to meet danger and fear with similar courage, confidence, and perseverance.

And so I say to you, my friend: *Let your courage rise with danger. Let your courage rise with danger. Let your courage rise with danger.*

Through exploring these habits and then systematically putting them into practice in your daily life, it is my hope that you will come to know and feel that you do, indeed, have within you the power to open your heart, to make the choice—day after day—to put fear behind you and live a full and blessed life. You already have that power dwelling in the core of your being.

These 8 Habits of Love will help you say good-bye to those things that make you more bland than spicy, more dull than bright. You will say good riddance to grudges, and certainly to the places where you have not forgiven yourself or where you haven't forgiven others. Old resentments, the self-defeating desire to be perfect, the desire to keep everything the way it used to be—these will become part of what *was* rather than what *is*.

It is so easy for us to get rigidly attached to our fantasies and our expectations about the way life should be. How easily those attachments block our ability to trust that we can live a life of love rather than fear. Our blueprints are so tightly laid out for our lives that we are often blind to the blessings and the newness that the Beloved has already placed right in front of us for us to enjoy. In opening our hearts, we open our minds and learn to let go of the old and invite in the new. Letting go of that which makes us stale instead of fresh and worn instead of energized helps us make room for newness and change. Upon closing this book, make your deepest resolution this: to live every moment in the *now* of *love*. To say to every person you encounter "I love you," so that they can say back to you, "I love you too."

On Sunday mornings I drive to work at six a.m., and as soon as I pull out of my driveway I turn my radio dial to KPFK to listen to the program *Gospel Classics*. Edna Tatum spins those songs and often between them she'll bark, "Get up, get up, get up! Wake up, wake up, wake up!"

When you wake up and catch yourself stale, timeworn, and half asleep because you are regretting or resenting something in the past or you are worried or fearful about something that is not even here yet, *wake up, wake up, wake up* and live in the now of love.

Finally, my friend, I want to share one of my favorite stories with you. Once upon a time there was a little boy who showed a great deal of promise as a piano player. His mother decided she would buy tickets to a concert so he could learn from a master musician. They went to a large concert hall where the great Polish pianist, Ignacy Jan Paderewski, was playing that afternoon. After they were seated, the mother spotted a friend in the audience on the other side of the hall. She excused herself from her son for just a second to walk over and say hello.

Now, this little boy was a curious tyke. So he decided to get up and explore the wonders of the music hall on his own. Of course, he was particularly attracted to a door that had over it a sign: NO AD-MITTANCE.

When the lights dimmed and the concert was about to begin,

the mother rushed back to her seat. All in the same instant, she discovered that her child was missing, the curtains were parting, the spotlight was focusing on a very impressive Steinway in the middle of the stage—and, in horror, she saw that her son was sitting at the keyboard, innocently plunking out "Twinkle, Twinkle, Little Star."

The great piano master tiptoed in, turned to the audience, put his finger to his lips as if to shush them, and quickly moved to the piano. He sat down on the bench by the little boy and whispered in his ear, "Don't quit—don't stop. Keep playing." Then, leaning over, Paderewski reached down with his left hand and began filling in the bass part. With his right hand, he stretched around to the other side of the child and he added a running obbligato. So, together, the old master and the young novice transformed a frightening situation into a wonderfully creative experience.

You and I are that child sitting at that piano right now.

The playing sometimes gets tough. You and I make mistakes; we become discordant. Yet whatever our situation in life and history, however outrageous or desperate, whatever dry spell of the spirit, whatever dark night of the soul, whatever temptation we experience to become cynical, however often we wonder how we will make it economically, we are not alone.

Love has taken a seat on our piano bench and is whispering deep within our being: Don't quit—don't stop. Keep playing. You are not alone. Together we will transform the brokenness of this world into a masterpiece of justice. Together we will enchant the world with our song of perseverance and of peace.

Permissions

Page 64-65: Andrew Bacevich

Page 109: Marvin Gaye
Stubborn Kind of Fellow

Page 151-153: Gregory Boyle

with permission of the author and Free press, a Division of Si-
mon & Schuster, Inc. All rights reserved.

Page 187-188: Alice Walker
Excerpt from THE COLOR PURPLE, copyright © 1982 by Alice
  Walker, reprinted by permission of Houghton Mifflin Harcourt
  Publishing Company. All Rights reserved.

Page 193: Amanda McBroom
THE ROSE (FROM "THE ROSE")
Words and Music by AMANDA MCBROOM
© 1977 (Renewed) WARNER-TAMERLANE PUBLISHING
  CORP. and THIRD STORY MUSIC, INC. All Rights Adminis-
  tered by WARNER-TAMERLANE PUBLISHING CORP. All
  Rights Reserved.

Acknowledgments

A multitude of colleagues, friends, and family members invested indispensable labor, support, and imagination in this book and its ideas. I am immensely grateful and indebted to each one of them.

My literary agent, Eve Bridburg, has become my reliable and trusted friend, confidante, and guide. At my side throughout this book's journey from idea to reality, Eve exuded vision, love, patience, wisdom, and good humor. Not only is she an extraordinary businesswoman, she is also a deeply intelligent thinker and an impassioned dreamer whose energy and insight infuse every page of this work. I am constantly blessed by Eve's faith in me and in this project. Stuart Horwitz, my book coach and developmental editor, engaged this material early at the level of the soul. His focused attention, his insights on the core components of a compelling book, and his vigorous engaging of the Habits in his own life helped bring muscle, sinew, and contemplative breath to this book. Katrin Schumann, writer extraordinaire, helped me bring the book to its final form when I had to concentrate my energies and time to the demands, challenges, and rewards of parish ministry. Katrin provided brilliant restructuring, captured my voice in a consistent and vibrant way, and brought my stories to even greater life with vivid detail and storytelling prowess. My editor at Grand Central, Karen Murgolo, took a giant risk when she included me in her circle of authors. Her kindness and firmly held standards infused this project with her grace and insight and gave fresh meaning to the word *imprint*. I also felt bolstered along the journey by Jamie Rabb's cheering genius. Deep bows of gratitude to all at Zachery, Shuster, Harmsworth Literary Agency, Grand Central Publishing, and Book Architecture. For all their detailed engagement in this book, I alone retain responsibility for any shortcomings and mistakes.

Fruitful life flows from a balance of solitude *and* community. I am indebted to the people, Vestry, and staff of All Saints Church, Pasadena, for supporting a four-month sabbatical spent mostly in solitude and to those supportive and inspiring friends who provided serene writing spaces in which my ideas were able to take wing: thank you to Adelaide Hixon, Ann Rutherford, Catherine Babcock, Rob Floe, Margaret Cunningham, Callae Walcott-Rounds, and Ed Rounds.

The eighth Habit of Love, Community, acknowledges that we cannot live a love-based life alone. Nor can one write a book alone. I certainly have not.

The ideas in this book were formed in the crucibles of loving faith communities, which include the Baptist Churches in the Wayne County, Georgia, communities of Odum, Gardi, and Altamaha; Benton Chapel, Vanderbilt University; New House Church, Nashville, Tennessee; and the Episcopal parishes of St. Paul's (Macon, Georgia), St. Anne's and St. Luke's (Atlanta), St. Mark's (Dalton, Georgia), St. Andrew's Cathedral (Jackson, Mississippi), All Saints Church (Pasadena), and Dolores Mission (Los Angeles, California).

I am also sincerely thankful for the prayerful direction I have received from the sisters of St. Mary, the Society of the Sacred Heart of Jesus, the brothers and priests of both the Society of Jesus, and the Society of St. John the Evangelist.

I feel a grateful spiritual membership in the Jewish and Muslim faith communities of Leo Baeck Temple, Ikar, the Pasadena Jewish Center and Temple, and the Islamic Center of Southern California.

One reason I know the universe is kind and generous is because I am blessed by an abundance of affectionate, affirming, resourceful, and forgiving friends. I am grateful for the life-giving energy from Elsie Sadler, Joe Henry, Melanie Ciccone, Frank Alton, Saul Renteria, Daniel Sokatch, Dana Reinhardt, Greg Boyle, Madonna Ciccone, James Carroll, Alexandra Marshall, Greg Adams, Michael Lapsley, Marcus Borg, John St. Augustine, Elizabeth Lesser, Sharon Brous, Reza Aslan, Adam Schiff, Serene Jones, Farid Esack, Salam al-Marayati, Laila al-Marayati, George Regas, Mary Regas, Leonard Beerman, Julius Lester, Joan Willens Beerman, Ellen Marshall, Bob and Susan Long, Shira Friedman, Ari Friedman, Gerry Puhara, Russ Ferrante, Maher Hathout, Ragaa Hathout, Salonas Hathout, Eba Hathout, Stephen Asma, Oprah Winfrey, Guy Ritchie, Levon Henry, Lulu Henry, Charles and Anne Hooker, Tena Clark, Michelle Seward, Katie Gibson, Joshua Levine-Grater, Franci Levine-Grater, Ramona Ripston, Stephen Reinhardt, Jonathan Gross, Sam and Sharon Muir, Giles Fraser, Heather Church, Ray Wells, Nazir Khaja, James Lawson, Brendan and Allison Parsons, Steve and Donna Richey, Sheldon Epps, Monette Magrath, Jessica Kubzansky, Jose Badenas, Michael Kennedy, Scott Santarosa, Jihad Turk, Ken and Allison Chasen, Miranda Bartlett, Jon Condell, Don Baker, Bryan Kest, Susan Luff, Mickie Crimone, Michael Palladino, Carol Palladino, Gary Emanuel, Myrna Carpenter, Hannah and Russ Kully, Liz and Rhodes Trussell, Cathy Keig, Jim Hayes, John Sweetland, Margo Groves, Chris Looney, Rick Happy, Carole Lambert, Deborah Smith, Jolly Urner, Pamela Baker-Masson, Juan Mejia, Diana Carbajal, Almudena Bernabeu, Nico Van Alstein, Margaret Sedenquist, Charlie Rahilly, Will Watts, Kim Rosen, Lynda Merritt, Todd Donatelli, Phyllis Diller, Corny Koehl, Geneen Harston, Zelda Kennedy, Gary Hall, Christina Honchell, Carissa Baldwin-McGinnis, Keith Holeman, Jane Kaczmarek, Lynn Schmissrauter, Nader Eldahaby, Wilma Jakobsen, David and Heather Erickson, Sam Prince, Toi Perkins, Susan Russell, Louise Brooks, Jeremy Langill, Juliana Serrano, Tom and Catherine Connolly, Seamus and Mary Marlborough, Philip, Michael, and Bernadette Monk,

Sharalyn Hamilton, Anne Peterson, Byron Katie, Stephen Mitchell, Ron and Jane Olson, Patrick San Francesco, Stephen and Linda Jacobs, Laura and Cooper Thornton, Anna Davalos, Sally Howard, Brian Huff, Marcia Behar, Laura and Rupert Thompson, Adriana Lizarraga, John and Carol Thompson, Susan Adkins, Abel and Mae Ling Lopez, James Walker, Melissa Hayes, Amy Brenneman, Brad Silberling, Brad Whitford, Stan Alfred, Julie Campoy, Archbishop Desmond Tutu and Leah Tutu, Mpho Tutu, Richard Hearns and Pu Hearns, Mike Farrell and Shelley Fabares, Martin Sheen, Joseph and Bettye Hendricks, Tom and Myrl Trimble, Mike and Lynn Class, Mike and Priscilla Brown, Gloria and Don Pitzer, Edith Westcott, Ned Tipton, Matt Leum, Bill Bowers, Mary Wilder, Sam Lloyd, Henry Hudson, Bill Lupfer, Sam Candler, Frank and Elizabeth Allan, Jon Bruno, Mary Glasspool, Gene Robinson, Diane Jardine Bruce, Duncan Grey, Fred Borsch, Ed Browning, John Michael Morgan, Julie Lynn, Bill Deverell, Doug Smith, Valerie Batts, Felipe Garcia, Sarah Stearns, Chris Hedges, Robert Scheer, Ed and Andrea Wills, Joyce Simmons, Jim Crawford, Randy Jefferson, Susan Brown, Jan Rutiz, Andy Delscamp, Margaret Burdge, Liz Morton, Peggy Phelps, Margaret Sedenquist, Laurie Zeh, MaryAnn and John Ahart, Tony Shalhoub, Brooke Adams, Trula Worthy-Clayton, Maria DiMassa, Joe DiMassa, Rich Llewellyn, Anina Minotto, Becky Thyne, Dick Patterson, Greg Stephens, Charlie McBride, Katharine Harrington, Lorna Miller, Scott Richardson, Sagrario Nunez, Bear Ride, Susan Craig, Vernon and Pat Loeb, Arianna Huffington, Kevin McDowell, Ken Turan, Terrence Roberts, Tom Hayden, Jane Dixon, Naim Ateek, Jenny Price, Chris Caldwell, Cam Sanders, Connie Smith, Bob Egelston, Marshall Rutter, Terry Knowles, Judith Fischer, Joseph Prabhu, Javier Stauring, Gabriel Stauring, George and Gretel Stephens, Michael Beckwith, Susan Caldwell, Nancy Moss, Fairfax and Kathee Randolph, Jim Fielding, Ken Wong, Robert Winter, Sharon Gelman, Susannah Heschel, Gloria Walker, Rocky Wade, Neil Comess-Daniels, Denise Eger, Suzy

Marks, Shakeel Syed, Aryeh Cohen, Shawn Landres, Aziza Hasan, Eric Greene, Tiffany Square, Jeff Denham, Rick Thyne, Chip Marble, Amada McCormick, Isabel Leus, Norma Guerra, Dan Matthews, Cathy Maginn, Adriana Lizarraga, Mary Jo Briggs, Roxie Bates, Ana Camacho, Szymon Grab, Michael Seel, the staff of Harpo Radio, Harpo Productions, and Oprah.com, and my colleagues, past and present, from Urban/Suburban Clergy Conference.

During the writing of this book my wife, Hope, broke her leg. Wonderful friends helped care for her so that I could work my day job at All Saints as well as spend my "off hours" writing. They thus made a contribution to this book that was invaluable. Deep gratitude goes to Victor Kenyon Brown, Beth Houskamp, Gayle Lowry, Christian Foster, and Lisa van Scoter.

For the past 17 years, the efficient organizer in my life has been my administrative assistant, Maren Tompkins. She is consistently the calm center of graciousness in my busy and often chaotic life, and for this I am greatly appreciative.

My mother, Nanelle Surrency Bacon, is the unsung star of this book. She embodies all eight of the Habits of Love for my loving brother, Will, me, and our families. Mother is the most positive person I have ever known. She believes that "family is better than medicine." I am grateful to her, her five siblings, and their families. My Surrency cousins and my Bacon cousins are among the most precious relationships I will ever have.

My wife, Hope, and I are the beneficiaries of two endlessly joy-filled friendships with our daughter and son, Alice Bacon LaGrone and Peter Edwin Merton Bacon. We are so grateful they were born to us three decades ago. We are even more delighted that they are our best friends now. Their spouses, Heath and Julie, and our grandchildren, Sarah and Luke, provide abundant enrichment.

The central relationship of my life is with a woman who has given me absolutely no benefit of the doubt in any philosophical, religious, spiritual, or truth claim I have ever made. Hope has been my steadying point of reference, unconditional source of love, and soul friend since 1968. I love her irreverent reverence. I am honored and moved to have a book that I can dedicate to her. It is a modest and visible sign of the transformative and ongoing adventure with her that still takes my breath away to this day.

Author's Note

In this book I am sharing stories of friends, parishioners, and colleagues where they can help illustrate my beliefs and advice. When only first names are used in stories in this book, the names have been changed to protect the privacy of the individual. In a few cases, the stories are composites of anecdotes from people whose stories were very similar. When a first and last name are mentioned in a story, the name is real.

References

Abadian, Sousan, and Tamar Miller. "Taming the Beast: Trauma in Jewish Religious and Political Life." *Journal of Jewish Communal Service*, Volume: 83; Issue: 2; Spring 2008.

Abil-Kheir, Shaikh. *Nobody, Son of Nobody*. Prescott, AZ: Hohm Press, 2001.

Bacevich, Andrew. *Washington Rules: America's Path to Permanent War*. New York: Metropolitan Books, 2010, 3.

Bloomfield, Harold, and Philip Goldberg. *Making Peace with Your Past*. New York: HarperCollins, 2001, 43.

Boyle, Gregory. *Tattoos on the Heart: The Power of Boundless Compassion*. New York: Free Press, 2010, 88, 94.

Camus, Albert. *Notebooks 1935–1942*. New York: Marlowe & Co., 1996, 13.

Coffin, William Sloane. *The Collected Sermons of William Sloane Coffin; The Riverside Years*, Volumes 1 and 2. Louisville, KY: Westminster John Knox Press, 2008, 68, 459, 575.

Dickinson, Emily. *The Complete Poems of Emily Dickinson*. New York: Back Bay Books, 1976.

Domino, Connie. *The Law of Forgiveness*. New York: Berkley Books, 2009, 45.

Donne, John. *Devotions: Upon Emergent Occasions, Together with Death's Duel*. Ann Arbor, MI: University of Michigan Press, 1959.

"Eva Kor (Holocaust)," The Forgiveness Project, http://theforgivenessproject.com/stories/eva-kor-poland/.

Filkins, Dexter. "A School Bus for Shamsia." *The New York Times*, August 17, 2009.

Finley, Guy. *The Seeker, the Search, the Sacred: Journey to the Greatness Within*. San Francisco: Weiser Books, 2011, 65.

Finneran, Richard J., ed. *The Yeats Reader*. New York: Scribner, 1997.

Grater, Rabbi Joshua Levine. "We Are All God Carriers: The Universal Wisdom of Archbishop Desmond Tutu." *Huffington Post*, February 26, 2011. http://www.huffingtonpost.com /mobileweb/2011/02/26/what-i-learned-from-desmo_n_ 828388.html.

Grossman, Lev. "Jonathan Franzen: Great American Novelist." *Time Magazine*, August 12, 2010.

Hafiz. *I Heard God Laughing: Poems of Hope and Joy*. New York: Penguin (Non-classics), 2006.

Harvey, Andrew. *The Hope: A Guide to Sacred Activism*. Carlsbad, CA: Hay House, 2009.

Hathout, Dr. Maher. Unpublished speech given at Los Angeles City Hall, September 11, 2011.

Heschel, Abraham Joshua. *Moral Grandeur and Spiritual Audacity: Essays*. New York: Farrar, Straus, and Giroux, 1997, 342.

Hoff, Benjamin. *The Tao of Pooh*. New York: Penguin, 1983.

King, Martin Luther Jr. *A Testament of Hope: The Essential Writings and Speeches of Martin Luther King Jr.* Edited by James M. Washington. New York: HarperOne, 1990, 269.

Kinnell, Galway. *A New Selected Poems*. New York: Mariner Books, 2001.

Logelin, Matt. *Two Kisses for Maddy*. New York: Grand Central Publishing, 2011, 140.

Machado, Antonio. "Last Night while I Was Sleeping" ["*Anoche cuando dormía*"]. Translated by the author.

McBroom, Amanda. "The Rose." www.amcbroom.com/rose.html.

Merton, Thomas. *Conjectures of a Guilty Bystander*. Garden City, NY: Doubleday, 1966, 140–41.

Merton, Thomas. *New Seeds of Contemplation*. New York: New Directions Publishing, 2007, 30–32.

Mitchell, Stephen (translator). *Tao Te Ching: A New English Version*. New York: HarperCollins, 1994.

O'Donohue, John. *To Bless the Space between Us*. New York: Doubleday, 2008, 185, 208.

Oliver, Mary. *American Primitive*. New York: Back Bay Books, 1983.

Rosen, Kim. *Saved by a Poem: The Transformative Power of Words*. Carlsbad, CA: Hay House Publishers, 2009.

Senge, Peter M., C. Otto Scharmer, Joseph Jaworski, and Betty Sue Flowers. *Presence: Human Purpose and the Field of the Future*. New York: Crown Business, 2008.

Smith, Dennis. *A Decade of Hope: Stories of Grief and Endurance from 9/11 Families*. New York: Viking Adult, 2011 (Kindle edition).

Tippett, Krista. *Einstein's God: Conversations about Science and the Human Spirit*. New York: Penguin Books, 2010, 215.

Tippett, Krista. "The Inner Landscape of Beauty," radio interview of John O'Donohue. *Speaking of Faith*, February 28, 2008.

Twain, Mark. *The Adventures of Huckleberry Finn*, a Norton Critical Edition, edited by Thomas Cooley. New York: W. W. Norton & Company, 1998, 223.

Walker, Alice. *The Color Purple*. New York: Harcourt, 1982.

Woodruff, Robert W. Foundation website: http://www.woodruff.org/bio_rww.aspx.

Yancey, Philip. *Rumors of Another World: What on Earth Are We Missing?* Grand Rapids, MI: Zondervan, 2003 (Kindle edition).

John 8:32 (NIV)

Luke 23:34 (NRSV)

Luke 17:21 (NKJV)

Matthew 18:3 (NRSV)

2 Samuel 12:7, 9 (NRSV)

Going Deeper

For those readers who would like to learn more about the values, ideas, and thinkers undergirding this book, the list of references at the end of this volume is an excellent place to start. Here are some additional insightful books and websites that helped me develop my personal philosophy of living a life based in love, not fear. I offer the following not as a comprehensive bibliography, but as a resource for those who would like to go deeper.

Books on Brain Science

Friedman, Edwin H. *A Failure of Nerve: Leadership in the Age of the Quick Fix*. New York: Seabury Books, 2007.

Hanson, Rick. *Buddha's Brain: The Practical Neuroscience of Happiness, Love and Wisdom*. New York: New Harbinger Publications, 2009.

Karr-Morse, Robin. *Scared Sick: The Role of Childhood Trauma in Adult Disease*. New York: Basic Books, 2012.

Siegel, Daniel J., and Tina Payne Bryson. *The Whole-Brain Child: 12 Revolutionary Strategies to Nurture Your Child's Developing Mind, Survive Everyday Parenting Struggles, and Help Your Family Thrive*. New York: Delacorte Press, 2011.

Other Invaluable Sources

Armstrong, Karen. *Twelve Steps to a Compassionate Life*. New York: Borzoi Books, 2010.

Aslan, Reza. *No God but God: The Origins, Evolution, and Future of Islam*. New York: Random House, 2005. See also http://rezaaslan.com/.

Borg, Marcus. *The Heart of Christianity*. New York: HarperOne, 2004. See also http://www.marcusjborg.com/.

Borg, Marcus, and John Dominic Crossan. *The First Paul: Reclaiming the Radical Visionary behind the Church's Conservative Icon*. New York: HarperOne, 2009. See also http://www.johndominiccrossan.com/.

Bourgeault, Cynthia. *Centering Prayer and Inner Awakening*. Cambridge, MA: Cowley Publications, 2004.

Carroll, James. *Constantine's Sword: The Church and the Jews*. New York: Houghton Mifflin Harcourt, 2001. See also http://www.jamescarroll.net/JAMESCARROLL.NET/Welcome.html.

Csikszentmihalyi, Mihaly. *Flow: The Psychology of Optimal Experience*. New York: Harper Perennial Modern Classics, 2008.

The Forgiveness Project. http://theforgivenessproject.com/. [Collects and shares real stories of forgiveness and conflict resolution and helps individuals transform the pain and conflict in their own lives.]

Hedges, Chris. "Acts of Love." Truthdig. http://www.truthdig.com/report/item/acts_of_love_20120219/. See also his columns at http://www.truthdig.com.

Hope Africa; Episcopal Relief and Development. http://www
.hopeafrica.org.za/contact.html and http://www.
er-d.org/. [Two relief and development organizations that are
on the ground everywhere there is pain.]

Keating, Thomas. *Intimacy with God: An Introduction to Centering Prayer*. New York: The Crossroad Publishing Company, 2009.

Keating, Thomas. *Open Mind, Open Heart: The Contemplative Dimension of the Gospel*. New York: Continuum Publishers, 1994.

Lesser, Elizabeth. *Broken Open: How Difficult Times Can Help Us Grow*. New York: Villard, 2005. See also
http://www.elizabethlesser.net/.

Merton, Thomas. *Essential Writings*, Modern Spiritual Masters Series. New York: Orbis Books, 2000. See also
http://www.merton.org/.

Merton, Thomas, and Robert Inchausti. *Seeds*. Boston:
Shambhala, 2002.

Mitchell, Stephen. *The Gospel According to Jesus: A New Translation and Guide to His Essential Teaching for Believers and Unbelievers*. New York: HarperCollins, 1991. See also
http://www.stephenmitchellbooks.com/.

Newell, John Philip. *Christ of the Celts: The Healing of Creation*.
San Francisco: Jossey-Bass, 2008. See also
http://www.salvaterravision.org/.

Nouwen, Henri J. M. *Lifesigns: Intimacy, Fecundity, and Ecstasy in Christian Perspective*. New York: Image, 1989.

Rohr, Richard. *Falling Upward: A Spirituality for the Two Halves of Life*. San Francisco: Jossey-Bass, 2011. See also
http://www.cacradicalgrace.org/richard-rohr.

Rosen, Kim. Poet, Author, Guide. http://kimrosen.net/.

Steindl-Rast, David, and Henri J. M. Nouwen. *Gratefulness, the Heart of Prayer: An Approach to Life in Fullness*. Mahwah, NJ: Paulist Press, 1984.

Tolle, Eckhart. *A New Earth: Awakening to Your Life's Purposes*. New York: Penguin, 2008. See also http://www.eckharttolle.com/.

Tutu, Desmond. *No Future without Forgiveness*. New York: Image, 2000.

Tutu, Desmond, and Mpho Tutu. *Made for Goodness: And Why This Makes All the Difference*. New York: HarperOne, 2010.

About the Author

Ed Bacon has served as Rector of All Saints, an urban Episcopal parish in Pasadena, California, with over four thousand congregants since 1995. Reverend Bacon's radically inclusive message has attracted Christians of all stripes, Jews, Muslims, and atheists to the pews, and has inspired visits and friendships from such high-profile people as Desmond Tutu, Cornel West, Madonna, Arianna Huffington, Amy Brenneman, Brad Whitford, and Tony Shalhoub. Bacon has discussed twenty-first-century spirituality as a frequent guest and host on *Oprah's Soul Series* on *Oprah and Friends Radio* and has been a panelist in the "Spirituality 101" segment of *The Oprah Winfrey Show*'s Living Your Best Life series.

Bacon has been honored numerous times for his peace and interfaith work, including the Religious Freedom Award from the ACLU of Southern California and the Peace & Compassion Award given to him by the Islamic Center of Southern California. He lives in Pasadena, California, with his wife, Hope.

If you would like to share your story with Ed Bacon, please email him at ed@8habitsoflove.com.